# VIRGINIA

# DAILY DEVOTIONS FOR DIE-HARD FANS

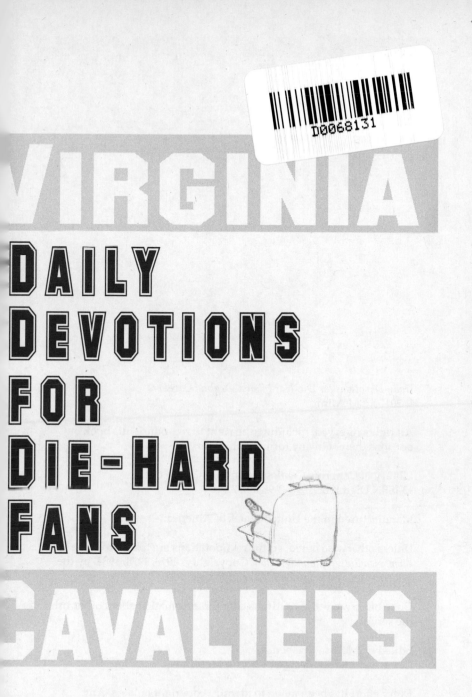

# CAVALIERS

*Daily Devotions for Die-Hard Fans: Virginia Cavaliers*
© 2011 Ed McMinn

Library of Congress Cataloging-in-Publication Data
13 ISBN Digit ISBN: 978-0-9846377-1-3

Manufactured in the United States of America.

Go to http://www.die-hardfans.com for information about other titles in the series.

Edited by Melissa Krispense
Cover and interior design by Slynn McMinn

Every effort has been made to identify copyright holders. Any omissions are wholly unintentional. Extra Point Publishers should be notified in writing immediately for full acknowledgement in future editions.

*Dedicated to*
*The Glory of God*

# VIRGINIA

## DAY 1

# IN THE BEGINNING

### Read Genesis 1, 2:1-3.

*"God saw all that he had made, and it was very good"*
*(v. 1:31).*

The Virginia "Eleven" beat up on would-be preachers and high-school kids in 1888, but it was the beginning of the football program that would rule the South for almost three decades.

After several years of playing around with a kicking game that resembled football, UVa in 1887 got serious by electing a former Princeton player, H. Reid Rogers, president of the "Foot Ball Association." Rogers assembled a team, played right tackle on it, instructed the neophytes on the game's finer points, and unsuccessfully tried to schedule a game with Richmond College. He did line up a game against Pantops Academy, a boys' school from across town. Charles Wilcox served as the captain of that 1887 club team, which debuted with a scoreless tie. A second meeting with Pantops in March 1888 resulted in a 26-0 UVa win.

Interest in and enthusiasm for this newfangled sport led to more organized efforts to field a team. On Nov. 20, 1888, Virginia launched its first official team, whipping Pantops again 20-0. Only four days later, the Virginians, captained by Francklyn A. Meacham, traveled to Alexandria and beat a squad of boys from Episcopal High School and students from Virginia Theological Seminary 16-0.

Buoyed by the two wins, the team invited Johns Hopkins to

Charlottesville for a game on Dec. 8. The 26-0 loss was Virginia's first regularly scheduled intercollegiate contest that could safely be called football. It also marked UVa as the first school south of the Potomac River to field a football team. That first season ended with the loss and a 2-1 record.

The 1889 squad, under team captain Sidney M. Neely, went 4-2 with wins over Pantops, Georgetown, Johns Hopkins, and Wake Forest. Football at the University of Virginia was on its way.

Beginnings are important, but what we make of them is even more important. Consider, for example, how far the University of Virginia football program has come since that first season. Every morning, you get a gift from God: a new beginning. God hands to you as an expression of divine love a new day full of promise and the chance to right the wrongs in your life. You can use the day to pay a debt, start a new relationship, replace a burned-out light bulb, tell your family you love them, chase a dream, solve a nagging problem . . . or not.

God simply provides the gift. How you use it is up to you. People often talk wistfully about starting over or making a new beginning. God gives you the chance with the dawning of every new day. You have the chance today to make things right – and that includes your relationship with God.

*The most important key to achieving great success is to decide upon your goal and launch, get started, take action, move.*
                                                           *-- John Wooden*

**Every day is not just a dawn;
it is a precious chance to start over or begin anew.**

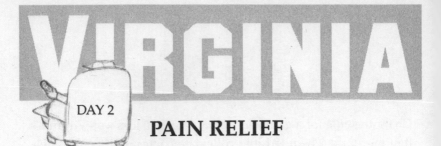

DAY 2

# PAIN RELIEF

**Read 2 Corinthians 1:3-7.**

*"Just as the sufferings of Christ flow over into our lives, so also through Christ our comfort overflows" (v. 5).*

**S**traight pain tolerance." That's what senior forward Will Sherrill said allowed him to come back from a broken bone in a simply unbelievable short time.

In August before the 2010-11 Cavalier basketball season, head coach Tony Bennett awarded the 6'9" Sherrill a scholarship. He had spent the last three seasons as a walk-on, starting seven games as a junior. His best game came against Cleveland State when he played 24 minutes and scored 18 points, grabbed six rebounds, and pulled off three steals, two assists, and a block.

Sherrill's versatility on the floor was vital to the team. On Jan. 2, 2011, for instance, he knocked down two 3-pointers in the closing minutes that helped seal a big 64-50 win over LSU. About that game: Both common sense and reasonable expectations would have told you that Sherrill wouldn't be playing that evening, let alone against Iowa State three days before. But there he was -- broken leg and all.

On Nov. 29, against Minnesota in the ACC-Big 10 Challenge, Sherrill had crumpled to the floor after the Gophers' 6'10", 258-lb. Colton Iverson fell on his leg. The post-game news was not good. Sherrill's leg was broken, his fibula fractured.

But there he was -- one month and one day later -- on the court against Iowa State. "He's the toughest guy on this team by far," said freshman K.T. Harrell in admiration. Sherrill just shrugged off any compliments, though he couldn't always ignore the pain. "It's just trying to man up, I guess," he said.

Manning up, Sherrill played in pain that required heavy taping and a fiberglass pad, that left him both hobbling and wearing an ice bag after practices and games, and that had him holding an electric stimulation kit on the leg when he was not in the gym.

Since you live on Earth and not in Heaven, you are forced to play with pain. Whether it's a car wreck that left you shattered, the end of a relationship that left you battered, or a loved one's death that left you tattered -- pain finds you and challenges you to keep going.

While God's word teaches that you will reap what you sow, life also teaches that pain and hardship are not necessarily the result of personal failure. Pain in fact can be one of the tools God uses to mold your character and change your life.

What are you to do when you are hit full-speed by the awful pain that seems to choke the very will to live out of you? Where is your consolation, your comfort, and your help?

In almighty God, whose love will never fail. When life knocks you to your knees, you're closer to God than ever before.

*The bone is healed enough where it's not really going to break more.*
    *-- Will Sherrill on playing a month after breaking his leg*

**When life hits you with pain, you can always turn to God for comfort, consolation, and hope.**

# VIRGINIA

## DAY 3

# TOLD YOU SO

**Read Matthew 24:15-31.**

*"See, I have told you ahead of time" (v. 25).*

Matt Schaub pretty much told his coaches, "I told you so," and neither they nor UVa fans could have been happier about it.

The Cavaliers opened the 2002 season with a 35-29 loss to Colorado State at home. Schaub started that game at quarterback and was benched after it, replaced by freshman Marques Hagans.

But Hagans struggled in the next game, a 40-19 blowout at the hands of 5th-ranked FSU that was pretty much over by halftime. In that game, Schaub got another chance. He left the bench in the second half and went 19 of 25 passing for 247 yards and three touchdowns. He never lost the starting job again.

Just as he had told the coaches.

"He could have made excuses early and blamed other people for his performance in that first game," head coach Al Groh said. "But when he was told he wasn't going to start the next game, Matt said, 'Whatever you decide I'm with you, but I can tell you when I get my chance again, you won't ever have to take me out.'"

It may have sounded at the time like the bragging of an athlete with wounded pride, but Schaub delivered. With No. 22 South Carolina in town for the third game of the season, the Cavs were in real danger of having the season get away from them. So Groh gambled and not just with Schaub. He started some of the younger players, such as future All-American offensive tackle D'Brick-

ashaw Ferguson and record-setting running back Wali Lundy.

Against USC, Schaub hit 20 of 30 passes for 170 yards and three touchdowns in a 34-21 upset. He led the team to a 9-5 record and a bowl win over West Virginia. He was named the ACC Player of the Year. As a senior in 2003, Schaub led UVa to an 8-5 record and another bowl. He set 22 school records, including career records for passing yardage, touchdown passes, and completions.

Matt Schaub had the last words: "I told you so."

Don't you just hate it when somebody says, "I told you so"? That means the other person was right and you were wrong; that other person has spoken the truth. You could have listened to that know-it-all in the first place, but then you would have lost the chance yourself to crow, "I told you so."

In our pluralistic age and society, many view truth as relative, meaning absolute truth does not exist. All belief systems have equal value and merit. But this is a ghastly, dangerous fallacy because it ignores the truth that God proclaimed in the presence and words of Jesus.

In speaking the truth, Jesus told everybody exactly what he was going to do: come back and take his faithful followers with him. Those who don't listen or who don't believe will be left behind with those four awful words, "I told you so," ringing in their ears and wringing their souls.

*[Matt Schaub's] resiliency was certainly the backbone of that team.*
*-- Al Groh on his 9-5 squad of 2002*

**Jesus matter-of-factly told us what he has planned:**
**He will return to gather all the faithful to himself.**

# VIRGINIA

## LIMITED-TIME OFFER

**Read Psalm 103.**

*"As for man, his days are like grass, he flourishes like a
flower of the field; the wind blows over it and it is gone.
. . . But from everlasting to everlasting the Lord's love is
with those who fear him" (vv. 15-17).*

Dick Bestwick's Cavs lost the 1976 Virginia Tech game 14-10,
but another loss resulting indirectly from that game was what
the head coach remembered most poignantly.

Bestwick coached the Cavs from 1975-81. He was an assistant
coach at Georgia Tech in 1971 when Marshall University hired
him as its head coach in the wake of the 1970 plane crash that
virtually wiped out the football team and the coaching staff. He
stayed in the position only two days before deciding to return to
Tech where he was coaching when Virginia hired him.

In the Tech game, UVa's Kevin Bowie, whom Bestwick recalled
as "a great kid and a good player," speared the Tech fullback. "The
one thing I never taught was spearing," Bestwick said. "Matter of
fact, I did the exact opposite." Bowie jammed his neck making the
tackle and couldn't practice the following week.

The Cavs' next opponent was Wake Forest in Winston-Salem,
and injured players didn't make the road trips. In the middle of
the week, Bowie asked Bestwick if he could use the weekend to
visit his grandparents in Washington, D.C. Bestwick told him,
"Yeah, that'd be fine, Kevin. Just take care of yourself."

# CAVALIERS

The Cavaliers snapped a long losing streak that weekend with a thrilling 18-17 win over the Deacons. Andre Grier, Bowie's roommate, made a spectacular catch for the winning touchdown late in the game. No sooner had the jubilant football team entered the locker room, however, than they learned from their head coach that Kevin Bowie was dead. He had been murdered the night before at a Washington-area McDonald's.

A heart attack, cancer, an accident, or violence such as a criminal attack will probably take -- or has already taken -- someone you know or love who is "too young to die," such as Kevin Bowie.

The death of a younger person never seems to "make sense." That's because such a death belies the common view of death as the natural end of a life lived well and lived long. Moreover, you can't see the whole picture as God does, so you can't know how the death furthers God's kingdom.

At such a time, you can seize the comforting truth that God is in control and therefore everything will be all right one day. You can also gain a sense of urgency in your own life by appreciating that God's offer of life through Jesus Christ is a limited-time offer that expires at your death – and there's no guarantee about when that will be.

*No one knows when he is going to die, so if we're going to accept Christ, we'd better not wait because death might come in the blink of an eye.*
*-- Bobby Bowden*

**God offers you life through Jesus Christ,**
**but you must accept the offer before your death,**
**which is when it expires.**

DAY 5

# CLOCKWORK

**Read Matthew 25:1-13.**

*"Keep watch, because you do not know the day or the hour" (v. 13).*

Because of the clock, no one -- not even the officials -- could tell whether or not the Cavaliers were NCAA soccer champions.

What is certainly the most exciting -- and the wildest -- finish to regulation in the history of major college soccer occurred on Dec. 8, 1991, when the Cavs met Santa Clara in the championship finals. The teams battled relentlessly all afternoon, and the match was scoreless as the clock ticked through the last minute.

But Virginia went on the attack with 11 seconds left. To the crowd's shock and amazement, midfielder Lyle Yorks lofted a pass to Richie Williams, who headed the ball across the goal mouth to Scott Champ, who in turn headed it into the net just as the scoreboard clock dropped to 0:00 and the horn sounded.

Immediately, the Cavaliers and their fans began celebrating, until folks began to notice that no official had made a call when the ball rolled into the net. The referee didn't signal a goal, but neither did he wave it off. Instead, he huddled with the lineman and the committee chairman.

At issue was whether or not the ball had crossed the goal line before time was up, as the rules required. Both teams and their fans waited anxiously for ten minutes until a ruling came. The goal was waved off. Television replays, which were not used in

the consultation, showed that the officials got it right.

So the teams played on and still refused to give any quarter. Sixty minutes of overtime later, the game was scoreless, the title to be determined by penalty kicks with the clock turned off. Coach Bruce Arena made a key strategic move by replacing goalkeeper Jeff Causey, who was battling the heat, with a fresh Tom Henske.

The move paid championship dividends when Henske blocked three kicks. UVa won the tiebreaker and the title 3-1. Finally, more than an hour after the clock first said it was over, it was over.

We may pride ourselves on our time management, but the truth is that we don't manage time; it manages us. Hurried and harried, we live by schedules that seem to have too much what and too little when. By setting the bedside alarm at night, we even let the clock determine how much down time we get. A life of leisure actually means one in which time is of no importance.

Every second of our life – all the time we have – is a gift from God, who dreamed up time in the first place. We would do well, therefore, to consider what God considers to be good time management. After all, Jesus himself warned us against mismanaging the time we have. From God's point of view, using our time wisely means being prepared at every moment for Jesus' return, which will occur -- well, only time will tell when.

*We didn't lose the game; we just ran out of time.*
– Vince Lombardi

**We mismanage our time when we fail
to prepare for Jesus' return, even though
we don't know when that will be.**

# VIRGINIA

### DAY 6

# WORRYWART

**Read Matthew 6:25-34.**

*"Therefore I tell you, do not worry about your life, what you will eat or drink; or about your body, what you will wear" (v. 25a).*

Y ou worried?" "Nah." "Me neither."

Such was the less than dynamic conversation between Cavalier wide receiver Herman Moore and tailback Nikki Fisher as they watched Wake Forest score two touchdowns in 46 seconds to take the lead. Sophomore fullback David Sweeney was a little more concerned. "You had to be thinking 'upset,'" he said. Considering everything that was on the line, Sweeney's anxiety probably was right in line with the way UVa's fans felt about then.

On Oct. 20, 1990, 6-0 Virginia took on Wake Forest on the road. The Cavs weren't just undefeated; they were ranked No. 1 in the nation for the first time in school history. They were 28-point favorites and looked it in jumping out to an early 9-0 lead. Suddenly, though, Wake hit a 60-yard bomb, recovered a fumble after the kickoff, and quickly scored to take a 14-9 lead with 9:15 left in the second quarter. The UVa offense was sputtering a little, apparently missing hospitalized All-ACC tight end Bruce McGonnigal. The defense was without leading tackler P.J. Killian, replaced by freshman Tom Burns, who had been designated for a redshirt.

Not to worry, said Moore and Fisher, which, as it turned out, was exactly the attitude to take. In the last 5:27 of the first half, the

# CAVALIERS

Cavs scored 19 points to make everyone's worries vanish. Moore himself got the scoring under way by hauling in a 49-yard bomb from Shawn Moore

By halftime, the Cavs led 28-14 and then scored again on the first possession of the third quarter. Later in the quarter, Fisher romped 63 yards for a touchdown. UVa won 49-14, finishing with 574 yards of total offense. The worriers should have listened to Moore and Fisher.

"Don't worry, be happy," Jesus admonishes, which is easy for him to say. He never had a mortgage to pay or teenagers in the house. He was in perfect health, never had marital problems, and knew exactly what he wanted to do with his life.

The truth is we do worry. And in the process we lose sleep, the joy in our lives, and even our faith. To worry is to place ourselves in danger of destroying our health, our relationships with those we love, and even our relationship with God. No wonder Jesus said not to worry.

Being Jesus, he doesn't just offer us a sound bite; he gives us instructions for a worry-free life. We must serve God and not the gods of the world, we must trust God and not ourselves, and we must seek God's kingdom and his righteousness.

In other words, when we use our lives to take care of God's business, God uses his love and his power to take care of ours.

*I can't be agitated every time we give up a pass or don't score.*
*-- George Welsh on not worrying after Wake Forest took the lead*

**Worrying is a clear sign we are about
our own business rather than God's.**

## DAY 7

# ULTIMATE MAKEOVER

**Read 2 Corinthians 5:11-21.**

*"If anyone is in Christ, he is a new creation; the old has gone, the new has come!" (v. 17)*

Football players pretty much have to make themselves over when they change positions because of the different skills that are required. Consider then Vic Hall, perhaps the most versatile player in UVa history, and the makeovers he underwent.

Hall finished his football career in Charlottesville in 2009, serving as a team captain and winning the team's John Polzer Award for ability, sportsmanship, and character. He was a prolific passing quarterback in high school, but after being redshirted in 2005, he was moved by head coach Al Groh to cornerback because the team was so thin there. He played in all twelve games, but he wasn't just a cornerback. He was also in on punt coverage on special teams.

Hall was a starting cornerback in 2007 and again played on special teams, adding punt and kickoff returning to his resume. He took on the additional duty of holding on place kicks and even scored a touchdown on a fake field goal. In one game, he lined up at running back, took an option pitch, and completed a pass.

Cornerback. Kickoff returns. Punt returns. Holder. Hall did them all in 2008 -- and more. In the last game of the season, against Virginia Tech, he returned to his roots. He started at quarterback and nearly led the Cavs to an upset, rushing for 109 yards and two touchdowns on runs of 40 and 16 yards.

Was there anything else for Hall to do? Well, yes. In 2009, he was a starter at safety for the first time. In the 16-3 win over UNC, he lined up at slotback and caught a pass. The following week he caught six passes, one for a touchdown, in the 47-7 beatdown of Indiana. Just for the fun of it, he also had a punt return for a touchdown against Boston College, but a penalty nullified it.

"He's really a significant athlete," Groh said about the Cavalier who repeatedly made himself over for the team.

Ever considered a makeover? TV shows show us how changes in clothes, hair, and makeup and some weight loss can radically alter the way a person looks. But these changes are only skin deep. Even with a makeover, the real you — the person inside — remains unchanged. How can you make over that part of you?

By giving your heart and soul to Jesus -- just as you give up your hair to the makeover stylist. You won't look any different; you won't dance any better; you won't suddenly start talking smarter. The change is on the inside where you are brand new because the model for all you think and feel is now Jesus. He is the one you care about pleasing. Made over by Jesus, you realize that gaining his good opinion — not the world's — is all that really matters. And he isn't the least interested in how you look but how you act.

*What hasn't he done for us? And he's always looked athletic.*
*-- Al Groh on Vic Hall*

**Jesus is the ultimate makeover artist; he can make you over without changing the way you look.**

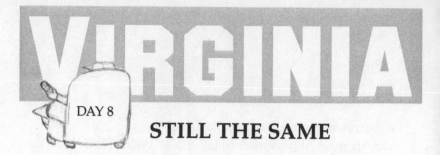

# STILL THE SAME

Read Hebrews 13:5-16.

*"Jesus Christ is the same yesterday and today and forever" (v. 8).*

**S**ome historians insist that a single shot changed everything about Virginia men's basketball.

The opening of University Hall in 1965 brought with it a new sense of optimism for a basketball program that hadn't been a consistent winner. "The facilities were just 10 times better," said Jim Connelly, who averaged 19.5 points per game from 1965-67, third best in school history.

But the new building didn't translate into wins. When Jim Hobgood enrolled in 1969, his mother came to a freshman game to watch him play. According to Hobgood, a three-year letterman who spent 12 seasons as the analyst for the Cavalier basketball network, his mother spent most of the game in the mezzanine stressing over sending her son to a place where the fans didn't show up and the teams lost. Barry Parkhill, a star guard and later an associate athletics director, came to Virginia in large part to prove that basketball could be a winning sport at the University.

And then came the evening of Jan. 11, 1971 -- the night of "the shot heard round the Hall" -- against 2nd-ranked South Carolina. Parkhill hit a short jumper in the closing seconds to lift the Cavs to a 50-49 win, its biggest victory in history. After wins over Wake Forest and Georgia Tech, UVa was ranked in the Top 20 for the first time ever.

Hobgood said that in short order U Hall became a basketball hotbed. Where the students had sparsely attended games, soon they were camping out to get tickets. "Within a year or two, the whole dynamic of the program had changed," he said.

The biggest change of all was that the team started winning.

Basketball at UVa has certainly changed over the years, but so has everything else. Smart phones, IMAX theaters, computers, George Foreman grills -- they and much that is in your life now may not have even been around when you were 16.

You shouldn't be too harsh on the world for its transient nature, though, because you've changed also. You've aged, gained or lost weight, gotten married, changed jobs, or relocated.

Change in our contemporary day is so rapid that often it both bewilders and confuses us. We desperately cast about for something to hold on to that will always be the same, that we can grasp tightly and use as an anchor for our lives. Is there really anything in this world like that, that is impervious to change?

Sadly, the answer's no. All the things of this world change.

On the other hand, there's Jesus, who is the same today, the same forever, always dependable and always loving you. No matter what happens in your life, Jesus is still the same.

*I'm not too proud to change. I like to win too much.*
                                                    *-- Bobby Bowden*

**In our ever-changing and bewildering world,
Jesus is the same forever;
his love for you will never change.**

# THE RIGHT MAN

**Read Exodus 3:1-12.**

*"So now, go. I am sending you to Pharaoh to bring my people the Israelites out of Egypt" (v. 10)*

New UVa athletic director Dick Schultz was on a mission to find the right man to coach the Cavalier football team. The man he found has been referred to as "the savior of Virginia football." He found George Welsh.

Schultz knew quite well that he was trying to fill a position in a place that had become known as a graveyard of coaches. Thus, he needed someone special, a coach who had succeeded in another environment that frequently killed the careers of good and respected college football coaches. The U.S. Naval Academy was just such a place.

Welsh had succeeded there, becoming the school's all-time winningest head coach and taking the Midshipmen to three bowl games in four seasons. The Navy athletic director counted on his head coach never leaving, declaring he'd bought Welsh a head-stone and a gravestone. But while his boss may have desired it, Welsh hadn't made a lifelong commitment to the Academy. In the fall of 1981, he told Schultz that sometimes the time is right for a change in a man's career. That time had come for Welsh.

In December 1981, Schultz introduced his new head man to the press, the public, and Virginia's eternally hopeful fans. "If it's a graveyard, it's a pretty nice graveyard," Welsh said about the challenges facing him. He struck exactly the right note when he declared, "I didn't come here to win four games."

He didn't. In his 19 seasons, Welsh led the Cavs to "unprecedented heights" that included 80 conference wins, two league titles, twelve bowl games, 134 wins, and a stretch of thirteen straight seasons of at least seven wins (1987-99).

George Welsh was the right man for the job.

What do you want to be when you grow up? Somehow you are supposed to know the answer to that question when you're a teenager, the time in life when common sense and logic are at their lowest ebb. Long after those halcyon teen years are left behind, you may make frequent career changes. You chase the job that gives you not just financial rewards but also some personal satisfaction and sense of accomplishment.

God, too, wants you in the right job, one that he has designed specifically for you. Though Moses protested that he wasn't the right man, he was indeed God's anointed one, the right man to do exactly what God needed done.

There's a little Moses in all of us. Like him, we shrink before the tasks God calls us to. Like him also, we have God-given abilities, talents, and passions. The right man or women for any job is the one who works and achieves not for self but for the glory of God.

*I am now and will be forever a Wahoo.*

*-- George Welsh*

**Working for God's glory and not your own
makes you the right person for the job,
no matter what it may be.**

# COMEBACK KIDS

**Read Acts 9:1-22.**

*"All those who heard him were astonished and asked,*
*'Isn't he the man who raised havoc in Jerusalem among*
*those who call on this name?'" (v. 21)*

**W**ith six straight losses to the despised Hokies behind them, the Cavaliers of 1964 desperately wanted a win. They got it by pulling off a last-minute comeback with a drive for the ages.

After a decade of dominating Virginia Tech, UVa lost nine of ten in the annual grudge match from 1954-63. "The Cavaliers have once again fallen under the spell," lamented the *Cavalier Daily* after the tough 20-15 loss in 1962 in which Virginia fumbled inside the Tech ten in the last minute. Before the '64 game, the newspaper declared, "The fans at Virginia are tired of listening to excuses. There is only one thing that Wahoos rooters will accept tomorrow, and that is victory. Nothing else will suffice."

That was pretty strong stuff considering that the Cavs were 0-2 headed into the Tech game. Then in what had become somewhat typical fashion for Virginia fans, Tech seemed to have scored just enough points to win. Tech led 17-14 when UVa got the ball at its own 21 with only 1:21 to play.

But head coach Bill Elias had installed a pro-style offense that featured a number of rollout option plays to best use the skills of a trio of talented quarterbacks: Tom Hodges, Bob Davis, and Stan Kemp. The biggest of the bunch was the "exciting, colorful" Davis,

# CAVALIERS

a sophomore, who "displayed a knack for continually getting himself in trouble, but finding a way out."

Davis started the drive by flipping a screen pass to Roger Davis that went for 23 yards. He then found John Pincavage at the Tech 42. Another Davis-to-Davis screen carried to the 29 with 33 seconds left. With Hodges in, the Hokies pulled an all-out blitz, but Hodges scrambled and found Larry Molinari open for a touchdown with twenty seconds on the clock. The Cavaliers had a 20-17 win and one of their most exciting comebacks ever.

Life will have its setbacks, whether they result from personal failures or from forces and people beyond your control. Being a Christian and a follower of Jesus Christ doesn't insulate you from getting into deep trouble. Maybe financial problems suffocated you. A serious illness put you on the sidelines. Or your family was hit with a great tragedy. Life is a series of victories and defeats. Winning isn't about avoiding defeat; it's about getting back up to compete again. It's about making a comeback of your own.

When you avail yourself of God's grace and God's power, your comeback is always greater than your setback. You are never too far behind, and it's never too late in life's game for Jesus to lead you to victory, to turn trouble into triumph. As it was with the Cavaliers against Virginia Tech in 1964 and with Paul in his life, it's not how you start that counts; it's how you finish.

*Turn a setback into a comeback.*
*-- Former college football coach Billy Brewer*

**In life, victory is truly a matter of how you finish
and whether you finish with Jesus at your side.**

# JUGGERNAUT

### Read Revelation 20.

*"Fire came down from heaven and devoured them. And the devil, who deceived them, was thrown into the lake of burning sulfur, where the beast and the false prophet had been thrown" (vv. 9b-10a).*

To their surprise, the Virginia women's basketball team was getting blown out of its own gym. But then to their opponent's surprise, the timid Cavs morphed into a juggernaut and went on one of the greatest runs in the school's basketball history.

The Cavs expected a tough game when they opened their ACC schedule on Jan. 11, 2009, against Wake Forest. They were a gaudy 13-2 and were favored, but the Demon Deacons came in sporting a 12-2 record of their own. Nobody in orange and blue, however, expected what happened in the first half. "We did not scout this," admitted Monica Wright, the school's all-time leading scorer.

The Wake head coach decided to put some hands in the faces of Wright and Lyndra Littles, the first time that season they had been face-guarded. "We knew it was coming," Wright said. "We just didn't know it would happen this soon." It worked. Wright shot 2-of-13 in the first half; Littles was 2-of-7. The result was a 16-point Wake Forest lead with five minutes to go in the half. "They came at us. They didn't give us anything easy," Wright said.

But the Cavs were too good to shut down -- so they did the opposite. They cranked up their engines and started rolling, using a

pressure defense and rebounds to key a series of fast breaks. The results were -- well, they were juggernautian, to coin a phrase.

Coach Debbie Ryan went to a speedy lineup of Wright, Littles, and three freshmen: Ariana Moorer, Chelsea Shine, and Whitny Edwards. That lineup took off on a 7-minute run that included five steals and six defensive rebounds. The result was 24 straight points. Before the run was over, the Cavs had outscored Wake by an incredible 38-8. UVa whipped the helpless Deacs 77-59.

Maybe your experience with a juggernaut involved a high-school game against a team that went on a 38-8 run, a league tennis match against a former college player, or your presentation for the project you knew didn't stand a chance. Whatever it was, you've been slam-dunked before.

Being part of a juggernaut is certainly more fun than being in the way of one. Consider, for example, the forces of evil aligned against God. At least the Wake Forest women had a chance when they took the floor against UVa that January night. No such hope exists for those who oppose God.

That's because their fate is already spelled out in detail. It's in the book; we all know how the story ends. God's enemies may talk big and bluster now, but they will be trounced in the most decisive defeat of all time.

You sure want to be on the winning side in that one.

*I'd never been to a mercy killing before.*
*-- College basketball coach Benny Dees after a 101-76 loss*

**The most lopsided victory in all of history is a**
**sure thing: God's ultimate triumph over evil.**

# VIRGINIA

### DAY 12

# ANGER MANAGEMENT

### Read James 1:19-27.

*"Everyone should be quick to listen, slow to speak and slow to become angry, for man's anger does not bring about the righteous life that God desires" (vv. 19-20).*

George Welsh was one angry man by the time he arrived at the stadium.

For UVa's head football coach, the bus ride into Lane Stadium for the 1984 game against Virginia Tech was a long one -- literally. It wasn't just that he was especially tensed up, which he was. The season before, the Cavs had gone into the Tech game fresh off a 17-14 upset of 19th-ranked North Carolina that clinched a winning season. Then Welsh's team went out and endured one of the most embarrassing losses of his career, a 48-0 thumping.

Welsh couldn't escape the memory of that defeat on the drive to Blacksburg in '84. He saw a bumper sticker that read "Squeaker of the Year . . . Tech 48 Virginia 0." Welsh said, "I don't know if the players saw it, but we kept passing the car and getting passed, so I saw it about three times."

But the head man's blood didn't start to boil until the team picked up a police escort once the buses turned off the interstate. "The Virginia Tech police picked us up," Welsh remembered, "and it took an hour and a half, or some ungodly length of time, to get to the game." The escort kept the buses in the right-hand lane while cars flew past them. Welsh had no doubts it was deliberate.

# CAVALIERS

His suspicions were confirmed when they arrived at the stadium and the police dropped the team off in the parking lot and not at the gate. "We had to endure the insults of the Virginia Tech fans as we walked to the locker room," Welsh recalled.

The mistreatment and the insults must have made the whole Cavalier team angry. They upset the favored Hokies 26-23 in one of the program's pivotal games. (See Devotion No. 42.)

Our society today is well aware of anger's destructive power because too many of us don't manage our anger as George Welsh did. Anger is a healthy component of a functional human being until – like other normal emotions such as fear, grief, and worry – it escalates out of control. Anger abounds when the Cavaliers lose; the trouble comes when that anger intensifies from annoyance and disappointment to rage and destructive behavior.

Anger has both practical and spiritual consequences. Its great spiritual danger occurs when anger is "a purely selfish matter and the expression of a merely peevish vexation at unexpected and unwelcome misfortune or frustration" as when Virginia fumbles at its own five-yard line. It thus interferes with the living of the righteous, Christ-like life God intends for us.

Our own anger, therefore, can incur God's wrath; making God angry can never be anything but a perfectly horrendous idea.

*By the time we got to the stadium, I was furious.*
*-- George Welsh on the 1984 ride into Lane Stadium*

**Anger becomes a problem when it escalates
into rage and interferes with the righteous life
God intends for us.**

**DAY 13**

# NUMBER ONE

**Read Haggai 1:3-11.**

*"'You expected much, but see, it turned out to be little. Why?' declares the Lord Almighty. 'Because of my house, which remains a ruin, while each of you is busy with his own house'" (v. 9).*

The lacrosse national championship game or her wedding ring? Clearly, Marty Curtis had her priorities in order.

Curtis was in the stands in College Park, Md., when the Cavaliers met Syracuse for the national title on May 31, 1999. She had a special interest in the outcome because her son was Ryan Curtis, Virginia's All-America defenseman.

With 13 minutes left in the game, Virginia midfielder Hanley Holcomb scored to put the Cavaliers ahead 10-4, a margin that seemed to pretty much turn out the lights on Syracuse's hopes. Suddenly, though, the Orangemen scored five goals in the next ten minutes; with three minutes left, the score was 10-9.

Virginia head coach Dom Starsia found himself experiencing some extremely unpleasant flashbacks. Twice before, in 1994 and '96, Starsia had seen his Cavs lose the national title in overtime. "We wanted the game to be over," he said. But it wasn't.

He wasn't the only one who was stressed at the time. Early in the quarter, Curtis realized that her wedding band was missing. "I'm seriously stressed," she said over the combination of the close game and the missing ring. But she had her priorities firmly in line. She remained in the stands watching the game while family and friends crawled under the bleachers and emptied rest room garbage bins searching for her ring. "I can't miss this finish," she explained. "You can always get another wedding ring."

Her son got his own ring as the Cavs held on to win 12-10 for the school's second national title. As fans scrambled for souvenirs, Marty Curtis had one of her own. She left the stadium with a bag of rest room detritus, hoping her ring was in there somewhere.

UVa lacrosse may not be the most important thing in your life, but you do have priorities. What is it that you would surrender only with your dying breath? Your family? Every dime you have? What about God? Would you denounce your faith in Jesus Christ rather than lose your children? Or everything you own?

God doesn't force us to make such unspeakable choices; nevertheless, followers of Jesus Christ often become confused about their priorities because so much in our lives clamors for attention and time. It all seems so worthwhile.

From God's standpoint, though – the only one that matters – if we work for ourselves and ignore our spiritual lives, we will never have enough. Only our deepest needs matter most to God, and these can be met only through putting God first in our lives. To ignore our relationship with God while meeting our physical needs is to travel down the sure road to death and destruction.

God – and God alone – is No. 1.

*I'm not having a good jewelry day, but I'm having a great lacrosse day.*
*-- Marty Curtis after the 1999 championship game*

**God should always be number one in our lives.**

# VIRGINIA

## DAY 14

# THE GRUDGE

**Read Matthew 6:7-15.**

*"If you forgive men when they sin against you, your heavenly Father will also forgive you. But if you do not forgive men their sins, your Father will not forgive your sins" (vv. 14-15).*

After the fiasco of the 1905 game (See Devotion No. 30.), Virginia and Virginia Tech held such a grudge against each other that they didn't meet again on the football field until 1923. They thus deprived their fans of what well could have been some of the greatest games in the rivalry's long history.

From 1906-22, both UVa and Tech fielded some of their greatest teams ever, among the best in Southern college football. The whole time, each school "stubbornly persisted in pretending the other didn't exist." During that 17-year period, the two schools won a combined 67 percent of their games. Virginia's record was a glittering 90-36-9; Tech won 96 games during the same period. "Clearly, the two schools were the best in the state of Virginia at the time, and their obstinance resulted in numerous missed opportunities for classic showdowns."

Part of the reason behind the longstanding grudge was that students and alumni, and not a separate athletic department, ran the football program at Virginia. Ill feelings remained strong in those groups. While some efforts were made to change the system, Virginia's success on the gridiron rendered such attempts futile.

Over the years, though, the attitudes on both sides mellowed a bit; at Virginia, a new generation of students couldn't recall exactly what had caused the breach.

Everything changed in 1923, when UVa hired Earle Neale, an outsider from the University of California, as the head coach. He had no emotional stake in the grudge, saw the importance of reviving the series, and immediately signed on to play Tech. Except for two years during World War II and a three-year period from 1967-69, the two schools have played each other ever since.

It's probably pretty easy for you to recall times when somebody did you wrong. Have you held insistently onto your grudges so that the memory of each injury still drives up your blood pressure? Or have you forgiven that other person for what he or she did to you and shrugged it off as a lesson learned?

Jesus said to forgive others, which is exactly the sort of thing he would say. Extending forgiveness, though, is monumentally easier said than done. But here's the interesting part: You are to forgive for your sake, not for the one who injured you. When you forgive, the damage is over and done with. You can move on with your life, leaving the pain behind. The past – and that person -- no longer has power over you.

Holding a grudge is a way to self-destruction. Forgiving and forgetting is a way of life – a godly life.

*There was too much feeling between the two teams.*
*-- Former Tech publicist Mel Jeffries on why they didn't play each other*

**Forgiving others frees you from your past,**
**turning you loose to get on with your life.**

# VIRGINIA

DAY 15

# PLAN AHEAD

**Read Psalm 33:1-15.**

*"The plans of the Lord stand firm forever, the purposes of his heart through all generations" (v. 11).*

**V**irginia head football coach Frank Murray came up with a plan for his 1941 football season that was considered so hare-brained that other college coaches snickered openly at the idea. The result was a season that tied the school record for wins to that point.

After the 1940 Cavalier season had ended, Murray took in the NFL championship game and watched the Chicago Bears use the T-formation to destroy the Washington Redskins 73-0. Duly impressed, Murray decided to alter his single-wing offense to take advantage of the T-formation.

That presented Murray with a serious problem, however. In the single wing, star tailback Bill Dudley, Virginia's first All-America, had been responsible for all the passing and kicking and much of the rushing. Playing him as a T-formation quarterback ensured he would be less effective because he wouldn't touch the ball as often. That's where Murray's unusual plan came in.

The coach decided to put Dudley in at left halfback when the team ran from the T-formation. When the Cavs needed to pass, Dudley would simply shift at the last second and take a direct snap. That set the coaches to chortling and shaking their heads. The plan would never work, they said, because it would take too long to teach it to the players.

# CAVALIERS

They were wrong; Murray's plan worked almost to perfection as the Cavs outscored their opponents 279-42. UVa went 8-1, only a two-point loss to Yale separating the team from an undefeated season. Dudley led the nation in scoring with 134 points and in total offense with 2,439 yards. He won the Maxwell Award as the country's best college football player.

Just as with success on the football field, successful living takes planning. You go to school to improve your chances for a better paying job. You use blueprints to build your home. You plan for retirement. You map out your vacation to have the best time. You even plan your children -- sometimes.

Your best-laid plans, however, sometime get wrecked by events and circumstances beyond your control. The economy goes into the tank; a debilitating illness strikes; a hurricane hits. Life is capricious and thus no plans -- not even your best ones -- are foolproof.

But you don't have to go it alone. God has plans for your life that guarantee success as he defines it if you will make him your planning partner. God's plan for your life includes joy, love, peace, kindness, gentleness, and faithfulness, all the elements necessary for truly successful living for today and for all eternity. And God's plan will not fail.

*If you don't know where you are going, you will wind up somewhere else.*

-- *Yogi Berra*

**Your plans may ensure a successful life;**
**God's plans will ensure a successful eternity.**

DAY 16

# HOLLYWOOD ENDING

**Read Luke 24:1-12.**

*"Why do you look for the living among the dead? He is not here; he has risen!" (vv. 5, 6a)*

Pure Hollywood drama. The greatest player in school basketball history was at the free-throw line in the closing seconds of the last home game of his career. His two shots would win the game. Perfect. Except that he missed both shots.

Ralph Sampson is almost a mythic figure among UVa fans. At 7'4", he was literally and figuratively the biggest college basketball star of the 1980s. He led the Cavs to their greatest run in history in a brilliant career that lacked only a national title. During the Sampson era, the Cavs were 112-23 and were ranked in the Top 10 for 49 straight weeks. He was three times the national and ACC Player of the Year and a four-time All-America.

It all ended for the home folks on March 6, 1983, against Maryland in Sampson's last game in University Hall. And it all came down to an ending complete with high drama and a twist just like something Hollywood would dream up. The whole night had a Hollywood touch to it as the ushers dressed in tuxedos and evening gowns as though they were at some sort of Tinseltown premiere rather than a basketball game.

With the Cavs down 81-80 in the closing seconds, Sampson was fouled and went to the line for two. Hit both shots, UVa would win, and just like in Hollywood, he "would ride into the sunset a

conquering hero." But then as the crowd gasped, Sampson missed the first shot. Okay, overtime. Then he missed the second shot.

Oh, but this was Hollywood, remember? Senior forward Craig Robinson got a hand on the rebound and tipped it back to Sampson. He took one step, shot, and nailed it. Ball game -- and the Hollywood ending was in the books.

The world tells us that happy endings are for fairy tales and the movies, that reality is Cinderella dying in childbirth and her prince getting killed in a peasant uprising. But that's just another of the world's lies.

The truth is that Jesus Christ has been producing happy endings for almost two millennia. That's because in Jesus lies the power to change and to rescue a life no matter how desperate the situation. Jesus is the master at putting shattered lives back together, of healing broken hearts and broken relationships, of resurrecting lost dreams.

And as for living happily ever after – God really means it. The greatest Hollywood ending of them all was written on a Sunday morning centuries ago when Jesus left a tomb and death behind. With faith in Jesus, your life can have that same ending. You live with God in peace, joy, and love – forever. The End.

*It was a great way to end a basketball game, and for me, it was a great way to end a career at University Hall.*

*-- Ralph Sampson*

**Hollywood's happy endings are products of imagination; the happy endings Jesus produces are real and are yours for the asking.**

## DAY 17

# BLESS YOU

**Read Romans 5:1-11.**

*"We also rejoice in our sufferings because we know that suffering produces perseverance; perseverance, character; and character, hope. And hope does not disappoint us" (vv. 3-5a).*

A thug put a gun to Mike London's head and pulled the trigger -- and it became a great blessing in his life.

On Dec. 7, 2009, London became the 39th head football coach of the Virginia Cavaliers. At the time, London had more than a decade of college coaching experience, but when he graduated from college, coaching was not part of his master plan. Instead, he became an undercover policeman. "We targeted rapists, robbers, beating subjects, guys who had jumped bail," London said.

After about three years on the job, London answered a robbery call one night. He located the van the thieves were in, and "like an idiot, I jumped in the driver's side while he was trying to drive away" and wrestled with the driver for control of the steering wheel. "That's when he pulls a gun, points it at my face," London recalled. "Looked like a big ol' cannon." But the thief didn't just point the gun; he pulled the trigger "and it went click."

When all charges were eventually dismissed in the case, London took a good, hard look at his life. "You know what?" he asked himself. "There's got to be something better than this because I just almost lost my life." The "something better" was coaching.

# CAVALIERS

When he joined the UVa staff in 2006, London showed up for media day wearing an earring. He explained it was a tribute to his daughter, Ticynn, who had battled a bone-marrow disease. She needed a transplant, but the odds that a parent could be a match were 10,000-to-1. London turned out to be a match, and his daughter went into full remission with a transplant.

Asked once to explain why he was so optimistic, London cited two great blessings in his life: that both he and his daughter had survived situations that didn't appear to be blessings at all.

We just never know what God is up to. We can know, though, that he's always busy preparing blessings for us and that if we trust and obey him, he will pour out those blessings upon us.

Some of those blessings, however, come disguised as hardship and suffering. It is only after we can look back upon what we have endured that we understand it as a blessing.

The key lies in trusting God, in realizing that God isn't out to destroy us but instead is interested only in doing good for us, even if that means allowing us to endure the consequences of a difficult lesson. God doesn't manage a candy store; more often, he relates to us as a stern but always loving father. If we truly love and trust God, no matter what our situation is now, he has blessings in store for us. This, above all, is our greatest hope.

*I've been blessed with my life being spared, and I've been blessed with my daughter's being spared with me as a vehicle.*
*-- Mike London*

**Life's hardships are often transformed into blessings when we endure them trusting in God.**

# MIRACLE PLAY

**Read Matthew 12:38-42.**

*"He answered, 'A wicked and adulterous generation asks
for a miraculous sign!'" (v. 39)*

**C**avalier tight end Jonathan Stupar was a walking miracle, but it took a loose screw to find that out.

Stupar was a three-year letterman (2005-07) for UVa who went on to start with the Buffalo Bills. He was redshirted as a freshman in 2003 and was expected to contribute in 2004. But he suffered a broken foot two days before the end of spring camp and underwent surgery. He returned to the field on Oct. 16 against FSU, in on 35 plays and catching one pass.

The following week, a routine follow-up revealed that a screw inserted in the first operation had come loose, requiring a second operation. "I was just crushed," Stupar admitted. "I was so looking forward to the remainder of the season." But as his father noted, the need for that second operation probably saved his son's life exactly because it kept him off the field.

The second surgery required a bone graft and an extensive convalescence that sidelined Stupar for the rest of the season. Shortly after the bowl game that ended the 2004 season, Stupar was in the weight room when he casually mentioned that he had fainted and had suffered a momentary loss of vision during the Christmas break. A trainer overheard Stupar's remarks; his reaction was "Hold on a minute."

Tests revealed Stupar's resting heart rate was more than three times the average rate. He had a heart condition so serious that doctors told him he had had a 90 percent change of dying in the time since his first surgery. Playing football for any extensive period would almost certainly have killed him.

Surgery permanently corrected the problem. When spring football practice started on April 1, 2005, Stupar was ready, no longer a walking miracle but just another young, healthy athlete.

Miracles defy rational explanation. Like playing even a single college football down with a serious heart condition. Or escaping with minor abrasions from an accident that totals your car. Underlying the notion of miracles is the idea that they are rare instances of direct divine intervention that reveal God.

But life shows us quite the contrary, that miracles are anything but rare. Since God made the world and everything in it, everything around you is miraculous. Even you are a miracle. Your life thus can be mundane, dull, and ordinary, or it can be spent in a glorious attitude of childlike wonder and awe. It depends on whether or not you see the world through the eyes of faith. Only through faith can you discern the hand of God in any event; only through faith can you see the miraculous and thus see God.

Jesus knew that miracles don't produce faith, but rather faith produces miracles.

*He's a walking miracle in my estimation.*
*— Jonathan Stupar's father, Steve*

**Miracles are all around us,**
**but it takes the eyes of faith to see them.**

## DAY 19

# JUST PERFECT

**Read Matthew 5:43-48.**

*"Be perfect, therefore, as your heavenly Father is perfect"*
*(v. 48).*

Perhaps accounting for her incredible success on the basketball court, Dawn Staley is a perfectionist. Just check out her socks.

Staley "is widely considered the best woman basketball player ever to emerge from the University [of Virginia]." In the four seasons from 1988-1992, the 5'5" guard led the Cavalier women to three Final Fours and one national championship game. She is the only basketball player -- male or female -- in ACC history to tally more than 2,000 points, 700 rebounds, 700 assists, and 400 steals. She set UVa career records in points (broken by Monica Wright in 2010), scoring average, free throws, and assists. She was the national Player of the Year both as a junior and a senior and was a three-time All-America.

Her play led coach Debbie Ryan to say, "Dawn is special to the game. God decided to make only one of her." Her high school coach said of Staley, who tended to be a loner, "She said hello at the beginning of the season, goodbye at the end, and in between, won all the games."

Staley honed her considerable skills playing against the boys on the playgrounds of North Philadelphia where she learned early on that if you passed the ball to the guys to shoot, you could play. She became so proficient at finding the open shooter that she

was usually picked for a team before some of the older guys.

Dawn Staley's drive for perfection on the basketball court was nothing new. When she was 3, her mom put socks on her, and she noticed that the red line at the toe of each sock wasn't straight. After her mother had her ready to go out, she sat down, took off her shoes, and straightened the red lines.

Nobody's perfect; we all make mistakes every day. We botch our personal relationships; at work we seek competence, not perfection. To insist upon personal or professional perfection in our lives is to establish an impossibly high standard that will eventually destroy us physically, emotionally, and mentally.

Yet that is exactly the standard God sets for us. Our love is to be perfect, never ceasing, never failing, never qualified – just the way God loves us. And Jesus didn't limit his command to only preachers and goody-two-shoes types. All of his disciples are to be perfect as they navigate their way through the world's ambiguous definition and understanding of love.

But that's impossible! Well, not necessarily, if to love perfectly is to serve God wholeheartedly and to follow Jesus with single-minded devotion. Anyhow, in his perfect love for us, God makes allowance for our imperfect love and the consequences of it in the perfection of Jesus.

*She was the perfect player.*
*-- High-school coach Tony Coma on Dawn Staley*

**In his perfect love for us, God provides a way**
**for us to escape the consequences**
**of our imperfect love for him: Jesus.**

**DAY 20**

# KEEPING THE PEACE

**Read Hebrews 12:14-17.**

*"Make every effort to live in peace with all men and to be holy" (v. 14).*

Virginia pounded Duke for three quarters, and then the real fighting began."

The Cavs were pasting the Blue Devils 28-0 after three quarters on Sept. 25, 1993. The home crowd was sitting on its hands calmly watching. On the first play of the fourth quarter, though, all that serenity disappeared as a full-fledged fracas broke out.

The instigator of the whole mess, interestingly enough, was Cavalier quarterback Symmion Willis. Apparently upset by an interception, he went linebacker and flattened the thief along the sideline in front of the UVa bench. A referee gave his flag a toss, and the Duke bench hurried across the field for something other than a social call. Pushing, shoving, kicks, punches, probably a few harsh words -- they all followed forthwith.

Some confusion reigned about what exactly started the brawl. Both teams agreed a whole lot of trash talking had been going on all afternoon. One of the referees, though, said Willis was indeed the catalyst: "He was on top of [the Duke player], wouldn't get off him and baited him verbally and by pointing at him. That's when everything broke loose."

When a semblance of calm was restored, the refs started looking for somebody to throw out of the game, and apparently most

# CAVALIERS

anyone would do. Two players from each team were ejected; one was UVa's Kevin Brooks. "I heard one official say to another, 'Give me some numbers,'" Brooks said. "I hadn't done anything. [I was] just there when they started looking for numbers."

Perhaps inspired by the brawl, the Cavalier defense proceeded to force Duke to punt -- and this is not a misprint -- on fourth and 58. UVa went on to win 35-0.

Perhaps you've never been in a brawl or a public brouhaha to match that in which the Cavs and the Blue Devils engaged. But maybe you retaliated when you got one elbow too many in a pickup basketball game. Or maybe you and your spouse or your teenager get into it occasionally, shouting and saying cruel things. Or road rage may be a part of your life.

While we do seem to live in a more belligerent, confrontational society than ever before, fighting is still not the solution to a problem. Rather, it only escalates the whole confrontation, leaving wounded pride, intransigence, and simmering hatred in its wake. Actively seeking and making peace is the way to a solution that lasts and heals broken relationships and aching hearts.

Peacemaking is not as easy as fighting, but it is much more courageous and a lot less painful. It is also exactly what Jesus would do.

*Somewhere some hockey player is going to be watching the highlights tonight and saying, 'Look at those football players.'*
*-- UVa defensive end Mike Frederick on the Duke brawl*

**Making peace instead of fighting takes courage and strength; it's also what Jesus would do.**

# VIRGINIA

## DAY 21

## NO GETTING OVER IT

**Read Ephesians 2:1-10.**

*"It is by grace you have been saved, through faith -- and this not from yourselves, it is the gift of God -- not by works, so that no one can boast" (vv. 8-9).*

When he was 10 years old, John Risher peeked through a second-story window and got his first glimpse of UVa football. He never got over it; right on through his 100th birthday, he was still involved with the team and the game.

It was in 1920 that the young Risher looked down on Lambeth Field and was snared by a lifelong passion. Actually getting in to see a game was a problem because of the 25-cent cost of a ticket. The savvy youngster got around that obstacle by landing a job selling sundries such as peanuts to the crowd. He gave that up only when he played high school football and got in free.

After high school, Risher stayed close to the Cavs by becoming the team manager. Then he caught a major break. "Coach Earl Abell, somehow or another, got the idea I could catch a football," Risher recalled. "I don't know where he got the information," but the coach asked his manager to come out for football because he wanted to throw the ball some. Fred Dawson became the new head coach in 1931; he didn't throw the ball much, but Risher was on the team anyhow his senior year.

After World War II, Risher completed his medical training, set up a clinic, and bought his first Cavalier season football tickets.

# CAVALIERS

More than sixty years later, he still had them. "I'm probably the oldest living season ticket holder," he said as he zipped on past his 100th birthday.

Risher very rarely used his seat, however, because he was in the press box keeping game statistics. "I keep track of where the ball is," he said, and "the distance of the drive, the time, and the plays. It's not a very big job, but I'm still a small peg in the group."

He just never got over Virginia Cavalier football.

Some things in life have a way of getting under your skin and never letting go. Your passion may have begun the first time you rode in a convertible. Or when your breath was taken away the first time you saw the one who would become your spouse. You knew you were hooked the first time you walked into Scott Stadium on game day.

You can put God's love on that list, too. Once you encounter it in the person of Jesus Christ, you never get over it. That's because when you really and sincerely give your life to Jesus by acknowledging him as the Lord of your life, God's love – his grace – changes you. It sets you free to live in peace and in joy, free from the fear of death's apparent victory.

When you meet Jesus, you're never the same again. You just never get over the experience.

*I'd always been interested in [football], but after I saw Virginia play, I loved it.*

*-- Dr. John Risher*

**Some things hit you so hard you're never the same again; meeting Jesus is like that.**

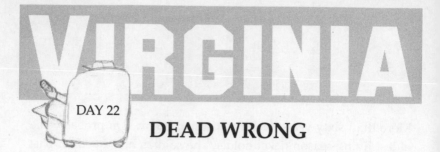

DAY 22

# DEAD WRONG

**Read Matthew 26:14-16; 27:1-10.**

*"When Judas, who had betrayed him, saw that Jesus was
condemned, he was seized with remorse" (v. 27:3).*

**J**ust a rich kid with a famous dad." "Soft and spoiled." Such
were the initial perceptions Clint Sintim had about a new team-
mate. He was both right and wrong.

Chris Long did indeed grow up as a rich kid with a famous
dad. His father is NFL Hall-of-Famer and sports commentator
Howie Long. Chris grew up in a big house in Charlottesville, his
life including summers in Montana and weekends in LA at the
Fox Sports studio with Terry Bradshaw and Jimmy Johnson. But
Chris is driven not by hardships as his dad was, but by his need
to counter the perception that because he had advantages, he was
soft and succeeded only because of his dad's name.

Thus, when he e-mailed linebacker Sintim to introduce himself, the response he received was not surprising. He didn't get
one. "I didn't really care for him," said Sintim, who knew Long
only by reputation. "I thought he was just a rich kid with a famous
dad. . . soft and spoiled." But Sintim, who led the nation in sacks
as a senior in 2008, quickly learned how wrong he was. The two
became roommates and such close friends that the Longs refer to
Sintim as their fourth son.

He shouldn't feel too bad about underestimating Chris, however; Chris' famous dad was wrong about him too. When Chris

tried out for his first youth football team, Howie told his wife their son would get hurt in the first practice and give up. When Chris survived that first day, Long told the coach he wasn't sure his son would stick with the game.

But Chris again proved his dad wrong. He was All-America as a senior in 2007 and won the Ted Hendricks Award as the top defensive end in the country. He became the first player in UVa history to have his jersey retired while he was still active.

There's wrong, there's dead wrong, and there's Judas wrong. We've all been wrong in our lives, but we can at least honestly ease our conscience by telling ourselves we'll never be as wrong as Judas was. A close examination of Judas' actions, however, reveals that we can indeed replicate in our own lives the mistake Judas made that drove him to suicidal despair.

Judas ultimately regretted his betrayal of our Lord, but his sorrow and remorse, however boundless, could not save him. His attempt to undo his initial wrong was futile because he tried to fix everything himself rather than turning to God in repentance and begging for mercy.

While we can't literally betray Jesus to his enemies as Judas did, we can match Judas' failure in our own lives by not turning to God in Jesus' name and asking for forgiveness for our sins. In that case, we ultimately will be as dead wrong as Judas was.

*I was obviously wrong about Chris.*
*-- Clint Sintim on his early perception of Chris Long as soft and spoiled*

**A sin is the first wrong; failing to ask God
for forgiveness of it is the second.**

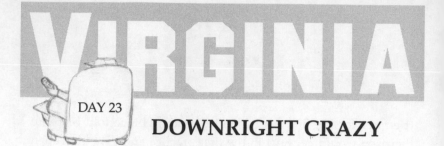

DAY 23

# DOWNRIGHT CRAZY

### Read Luke 13:31-35.

*"Some Pharisees came to Jesus and said to him, 'Leave this place and go somewhere else. Herod wants to kill you.' He replied, 'Go tell that fox . . . I must keep going today and tomorrow and the next day'" (vv. 31-33).*

**O**ur kid is crazy."

So spoke the father to his wife when he didn't get the results he wanted from his 9-month-old son. The dad was Andranik Eskandarian, who in 1983 watched in wonder with his wife as their boy Alecko suddenly stood up for the first time. The father knelt and implored his son to walk to him. Alecko would have none of it. Instead, he hauled off and kicked the daylights out of a Nerf soccer ball, eliciting the surprised but thrilled response from Andranik about the state of his boy's mental condition.

The dad had some immediate suspicions about what his son's crazy kick implied. They were confirmed when Alecko kicked a soccer ball through a window in the home; the boy was 16 months old. Something crazy was indeed going on, and Andranik knew what it was. A former star defender for the New York Cosmos, he shrewdly determined that his son had a special talent for soccer.

When Alecko was seven, the dad set up a soccer goal in the backyard. He taught his son the game's basics and then went inside. Three hours later, he spied Alecko "alone in the darkness, running around, pumping his fist and uncorking one shot after another toward the net." "That's when I knew he had a chance to be special," the dad said. He knew his son was crazy for soccer.

The younger Eskandarian brought that passion for soccer to Charlottesville in 2000 and became one of UVa's greatest players. In 2002, he won the Hermann Trophy as the best college player in the country. He set a school record that season with 25 goals, and his 54 points that season is second in UVa history only to Mike Fisher's 57 points in 1995.

And it all started with that one crazy kick.

What some see as crazy often is shrewd instead. Like the time you went into business for yourself or when you decided to go back to school. Maybe it was when you fixed up that old house. Or when you bought that new company's stock.

You know a good thing when you see it but are also shrewd enough to spot something that's downright crazy. Jesus was that way too. He knew that his entering Jerusalem was in complete defiance of all apparent reason and logic since a whole bunch of folks who wanted to kill him were waiting for him there.

Nevertheless, he went because he also knew that when the great drama had played out he would defeat not only his personal enemies but the most fearsome enemy of all: death itself.

It was, after all, a shrewd move that provided the way to your salvation.

*Football is easy if you're crazy.*

-- Bo Jackson

**It's so good it sounds crazy -- but it's not: through faith in Jesus, you can have eternal life with God.**

# VIRGINIA

## DAY 24

# SOUND OFF

**Read Revelation 4:1-10, 5:6-14.**

*"Then I looked and heard the voice of many angels, numbering thousands upon thousands, and ten thousand times ten thousand" (v. 11a).*

The Cavs pulled off one of the biggest upsets of their long series with Virginia Tech in 1970. But what one Virginia player remembered most about the game was the silence of the scoreboard.

The rivalry broke off after the 1966 game. At the time, the two football programs were headed in different directions. The Hokies had moved into 40,000-seat Lane Stadium for the 1965 season and had installed a $40,000 scoreboard that broke into a clamorous celebration when Tech scored. UVa's Scott Stadium meanwhile did not undergo major renovations until the mid-1970s. Indeed, the ACC's SAT requirements led many to question the league's commitment to athletics. Tech often brought in as many as fifty scholarship players a year while Virginia had only twenty or so.

Thus, even though the Cavaliers claimed they wanted to concentrate on conference games when they halted the series, the general perception was that they were dodging the Hokies. Still, lobbying to resume the rivalry began almost as soon as it ended. Money eventually won out. Tech athletic director Frank Moseley guaranteed his Cavalier counterpart, Steve Sebo, $70,000 if he would bring the Cavs to Lane Stadium in 1970. That led to a game that saw the Hokies established as prohibitive favorites.

Instead, the Cavs pulled off the upset. UVa defensive tackle Andy Selfridge led a magnificent defense that held Tech to 201 total yards and handed the Hokies their first shutout loss since 1962. Virginia won 7-0. Cavalier wide receiver Bob Bischoff had no problem recalling what was for him the highlight of the game. "We never did hear that $40,000 scoreboard of theirs," he said.

For the Cavs, silence told the story of the game.

Scott Stadium erupts in a cacophony on game day. Loud music blares from the speakers in the car next to you at the traffic light. The garbage men bang the cans around as though they receive bonuses for waking you up. A silence of any length in a conversation makes us uncomfortable; somebody please say something.

We live in a noisy world with all that racket indicating activity, busyness, progress, and engagement with life. The problem with all that noise -- however constructive it may be -- is that it drowns out the gentle voice of God. Thus, some quiet time each day is imperative if we are to grow in our relationship with God. The intentional seeking of silence in which to hear God's voice constitutes surrender to the divine.

Though much about Heaven will be strange, we should be quite comfortable there. Revelation's lengthy description of God's home makes it very clear that it's a noisy place reverberating with the inspiring, exhilarating, and awesome sound of worship.

*You can tell a good putt by the noise it makes.*
                                        *-- Pro Hall of Fame golfer Bobby Locke*

**Heaven is a quite noisy place, echoing constantly with the wonderful sounds of worship.**

# GOOD ADVICE

**Read Isaiah 8:11-9:7.**

*"And he will be called Wonderful Counselor" (v. 9:6b).*

With the game riding on his extra-point try in the closing seconds, Robert Randolph took his coaches' advice. And promptly had a defender get a hand on his kick.

Randolph was a redshirt freshman walk-on who had never put toe to leather in the heat of battle when an injury to another kicker pressed him into action against North Carolina on Oct. 18, 2008. Of course, the game came down to his kick.

Randolph hit his first field-goal try of the game, a 37-yarder in the third quarter that cut 18th-ranked UNC's lead to 7-3. Later in the quarter, though, a 39-yard attempt was blocked. When a flustered Randolph returned to the sideline, he received some coaching advice: Speed it up a bit, son.

The Heels led 10-3 when the Cavs got the ball on their own 18 with only 2:22 left in the game. Sophomore quarterback Marc Verica proceeded to complete seven straight passes, including a 26-yarder to Maurice Covington, a 16-yard chunk to Cary Koch, and a 17-yard completion to Kevin Ogletree.

With 47 seconds left on the clock, Cedric Peerman scored from the 2. Enter Randolph with his team trailing 10-9. "It was a real tense moment," he admitted. But he followed his coaches' advice and sped up some. Good thing. To the horror of UVa fans, a Carolina safety got his hand on the kick and deflected it. Because

# CAVALIERS

Randolph had hurried his kick, though, it was a deflection and not a block. The ball wobbled over the uprights to tie the game.

In overtime, Peerman scored again for a 16-13 UVa win.

Like Robert Randolph in his first game, we all need a little advice now and then. More often than not, we turn to professional counselors, who are all over the place. Marriage counselors, grief counselors, school guidance counselors, rehabilitation counselors, all sorts of mental health and addiction counselors -- we even have counselors for our pets. No matter what our situation or problem, we can find plenty of advice for the taking.

The problem with all this counseling is that we find advice easy to offer but hard to swallow. We also have a tendency to go to the wrong source for advice, seeking counsel that doesn't really solve our problem but that instead enables us to continue with it.

Our need for outside advice, for an independent perspective on our situation, is actually God-given. God serves many functions in our lives, but one role clearly delineated in his Word is that of Counselor. Jesus himself is described as the "Wonderful Counselor." All the advice we need in our lives is right there for the asking; we don't even have to pay for it except with our faith. God is always there for us: to listen, to lead, and to guide.

*I don't think you want to listen to what the fans say. If you listen to them too much, you'll be sitting up there with them.*
*-- Frank Beamer on taking advice from fans*

**We all need and seek advice in our lives,**
**but the ultimate and most wonderful Counselor**
**is of divine and not human origin.**

DAY 26

# SMILING FACES

### Read Philippians 4:4-7.

*"Rejoice in the Lord always. I will say it again: Rejoice!"*
*(v. 4)*

**S**ometimes, all you can do about it is smile. Even Dean Smith did one night while the Cavaliers thrashed his Heels.

North Carolina's Tar Heels had their usual spot in the Top 10 when they came to Charlottesville on Jan. 15, 1989. UVa would finish the season 22-11 and advance to the Elite Eight in the NCAA Tournament by knocking off top-ranked Oklahoma. When the Cavs met Carolina, though, they were struggling; they had lost five straight, were only 7-6, and were without head coach Terry Holland, sidelined by stomach surgery. "Nobody really gave us a shot to win the game," said first-year player Bryant Stith.

But on this night they had senior guard Richard Morgan. Morgan had a more than solid career for the Cavs. He lettered four times (1986-89) and was a three-year starter. He ranks eighth on UVa's list of career steals, tenth in career field goals made, and 15th on the all-time scoring list. He led that '89 Elite Eight team in scoring, free throw percentage, and steals.

No time during his career, however, was he more spectacular than against North Carolina. "Richard was, I mean, he was white-hot that night," recalled Carolina basketball broadcaster Woody Durham. How hot was Morgan? Well, on one occasion, he ran to save the ball from going out of bounds, turned when he got

possession, fired it in the general area of the net since he was falling out of bounds, and hit the shot.

Morgan hit eight of 15 three-point shots and scored 39 points, a career high. UVa was off and running toward a great season with a 106-83 win. "It was that kind of night," Morgan said.

One fan said he'd look over to Carolina head coach Dean Smith every time Morgan made another three, "and he would just laugh, because he knew that this wasn't Carolina's day. He knew that Morgan was on and couldn't miss. I think he enjoyed it as much as anyone else."

What does your smile say about you? What is it that makes you smile and laugh in the first place? Your dad's corny jokes? Don Knotts as Barney Fife? Your children or grandchildren? Do you hoard your smile or do you give it away easily even when you've had some tough times?

When you smile, the ones who love you and whom you love can't help but return the favor -- and the joy. It's like turning on a bright light in a world threatened by darkness. Besides, you have good reason to walk around all the time with a smile on your face, not because of something you have done but rather because of one basic, unswerving truth: God loves you. As a result of his great love for you, God acted through Jesus to give you free and eternal salvation. That should certainly make you smile.

*The bat is gone but the smile remains.*
*-- Baseball Hall of Famer Willie Stargell*

**It's so overused it's become a cliché, but it's true nevertheless: Smile! God loves you.**

### DAY 27

# TO BOLDLY GO

**Read Acts 4: 1-21.**

*"Judge for yourselves whether it is right in God's sight to obey you rather than God. For we cannot help speaking about what we have seen and heard" (vv. 19-20).*

George Welsh made a call in the 1999 BYU game that was so bold one writer called it "unthinkable."

On Sept. 25, the Cavaliers won a shootout with the 17th-ranked Cougars 45-40. Though UVa never trailed, the game was in doubt until freshman safety Jerton Evans pulled down an interception in the end zone with 1:37 to play. As it turned out, the game hinged on a Welsh gamble so unprecedented that the head coach of 27 years couldn't recall the exact circumstances under which he had ever before made a similar call. "I've probably done it before [but] not much," he said.

The Cavs, seven-point underdogs, were led by senior tailback Thomas Jones, who carried 35 times for a career-high 210 yards. UVa stunned the Cougar Stadium crowd by jumping out to a 21-0 lead in the first quarter. Quarterback Dan Ellis threw touchdown tosses to fullback Anthony Southern and wide receiver Kevin Coffey, and Jones ripped off a 23-yard scoring run.

But the Cougars rallied and cut the Cavalier lead to 38-33. Late in the third quarter, UVa faced a fourth and inches just inside its own 30. Welsh hinted that he might go for it when he checked with offensive coordinator Gary Tranquill, who would have none of the responsibility. "Your call," he told his boss. Convinced his defense couldn't completely stop the Cougars' high-flying offense, Welsh decided to go for it. He left the call up to Tranquill, who decided on a quarterback sneak. Ellis plowed forward for two yards behind mammoth center John St. Clair.

That bold call keyed an 11-play, 80-yard drive that resulted in what was ultimately the game-winning touchdown.

To act boldly is to take unconventional action that involves risk, as George Welsh did against BYU. We all at times in our lives act boldly. When you proposed marriage, for example. Or when you took that new job. We act boldly because we believe the reward justifies the risk.

Why is it then that so many of us who are confident and bold in our professional and personal lives are such timid little things when it comes to our faith life? Why are we so afraid to speak boldly of and act boldly for Jesus? Do we fear offending someone? Are we afraid of rejection? And yet we allegedly serve a Lord who went out of his way to offend the religious authorities and who ultimately was rejected unto death. If anything, Jesus was bold.

Our faith should be burning so strongly in us that we cannot help but live boldly for Jesus. After all, how can we expect Jesus to step boldly forward on judgment day and claim us as his own when we don't claim him as our own now?

*Does Coach Welsh know about it?*
*-- Thomas Jones' first thought when told the Cavs were going for it*

**We serve a Lord bold enough to die for us;
we should at least live boldly for him.**

# VIRGINIA

## DAY 28

# NIGHTFALL

**Read Psalm 74:12-23.**

*"The day is yours, and yours also the night; you established the sun and moon" (v. 16).*

The 2009 Cavalier baseball team was a bunch of night owls.

Coach Brian O'Connor's team discovered they liked playing at night when the NCAA sent them to Irvine, Calif., for the first round of the NCAA Tournament. The ACC champs were 43-12-1 and were ranked No. 6 in the country. Nevertheless, the NCAA powers-that-be mysteriously decided they didn't merit a top-16 seed and thus a regional at home. Instead of sleeping in their own beds, the players found themselves fighting jet lag, facing three straight 8 p.m. starts (11 p.m. back home), and battling a field so tough it was humorlessly called "the region of death."

O'Connor arranged the trip west to account for the time difference and the late starts by having the team fly out a day earlier than usual. That gave the squad an extra day's acclimation time, but the ACC tournament with its late starts also helped out. "The players had gotten into a routine where we'd have breakfast at a certain time, then they'd try and keep themselves busy the entire day," the head coach said.

No matter the hour, the Cavs were ready. In the opening game, they defeated San Diego State and the now somewhat legendary blazer Stephen Strasburg 5-1. Phil Gosselin, the second UVa batter of the game, hit a home run off the first pitch he saw.

# CAVALIERS

The Cavs continued to enjoy the night life by defeating the host team, top-ranked University of California at Irvine, 5-0 in their second regional game. They then avoided a fourth straight night game by beating UCI 4-1 Sunday night to sweep the regional. Senior Andrew Carraway and sophomore Kevin Arico combined for a four-hitter with Arico throwing the final pitch at 2:19 a.m. EDT. By then, the night owls from Charlottesville were quite used to playing ball long after the sun went down.

A rarity in the early days of collegiate competition, night games have become an accepted part of contemporary college sports. With the lighting expertise we have today, our night games are played under conditions that are "as bright as day."

It is artificial night, though, man-made and not God-made. Our electric lights can illumine only a portion of God's night; they can never chase it away. The night, like the day, is a gift from God to be enjoyed, to function as a necessary part of our lives. The night is a part of God's plan for creation and a natural cycle that includes both activity and rest.

The world is different at nightfall. Whether we admire a stunning sunset, are dazzled by fireflies, or simply find solace in the descending quiet, the night reminds us of the variety of God's creation and the need the creation has for constant renewal.

*When we lose, I can't sleep at night; when we win, I can't sleep at night. But when you win, you wake up feeling better.*
-- *Baseball manager Joe Torre*

**Like the day, night is part of both the beauty
and the order of God's creation.**

# IN THE KNOW

### Read John 4:19-26, 39-42.

*"They said to the woman, . . . 'Now we have heard for ourselves, and we know that this man really is the Savior of the world'" (v. 42).*

The Cavaliers stuffed the try for the game-winning conversion so brutally that it was like they knew what was coming. As it turns out -- they did.

On Sept. 19, 1987, senior quarterback Scott Secules completed his first seven passes, including touchdown tosses to Keith Mattioli and Tim Finkelston, as the Cavs jumped out to a 14-0 lead against Virginia Tech. The Hokies rallied, though, and with only 1:24 left to play, they scored to make it a 14-13 game.

Tech decided to go for the win with a two-point conversion. The tailback never even made it out of his backfield before sophomore defensive end Elton Toliver and fellow defensive end Jeff Lageman led a host of Wahoos who blew up the play to preserve the win. As one writer put it, Virginia's defense was in the backfield so quickly "they seemed to know the play." He was right.

After the game, Toliver admitted that one of the Tech linemen had tipped off the play before the snap. Virginia Tech tight end Steve Johnson was not at all surprised. "You would think, as quick as they jumped on us, something bad went wrong," he said.

Just exactly what did the Cavs see that put them in the know? "The guard had been leaning," Toliver explained. "Not terribly, but you noticed the tendency every now and then." Toliver spotted the "leaning" immediately prior to the snap on the conversion. On his own, he shifted to the guard's inside shoulder and shot through a gap. "It was all instinct," Toliver explained, adding, "I wasn't the only one back there."

Toliver said head coach George Welsh had warned him about such gambles, noting that while they paid off, sometimes the defense got badly burned. This time, though, because Toliver and his defensive mates knew where the play was going, the Cavs preserved a 14-13 win.

The Virginia defense just knew in the same way you know certain things in your life. That your spouse loves you, for instance. That you are good at your job. That a bad day fishing is still better than a good day at work. That despite all its foibles, this is still a great country. You know these things even though no mathematician or philosopher can prove any of this on paper.

It's the same way with faith in Jesus: You just know that he is God's son and the savior of the world. You know it in the same way that you know the Cavs are the only team worth pulling for: with every fiber of your being, with all your heart, your mind, and your soul.

You just know, and because you know him, Jesus knows you. And that is all you really need to know.

*I remember watching the play on film and just shaking my head.*
*-- Tech's Steve Johnson on the two-point conversion attempt in 1987*

**A life of faith is lived in certainty and conviction:
You just know you know.**

# VIRGINIA

# A SURE THING

**Read Romans 8:28-30.**

*"We know that in all things God works for the good of those who love him, who have been called according to his purpose" (v. 28).*

Relations between Virginia and Virginia Tech were so strained for a time that in 1905, even when the crowd showed up and the teams took the field, no one was sure the game would be played.

In the first eight meetings, UVa "mercilessly pounded" the Hokies, outscoring them 170-5. In 1905, though, Tech won its first five games behind a back who was playing his seventh season of college football in those days of rather loose eligibility rules.

Serious trouble had been brewing for some time as Virginia players groused that Tech was paying some of its players, including that running back. Early in the season, UVa's athletic managers had the Tech players sign affidavits that they were all eligible to play as amateurs. But then the week of the game, the Virginia student newspaper claimed the school's officials had "absolute evidence" that the star back was being paid to play. The paper said Virginia would not play the game unless that back stood "trial before a jury of unprejudiced men." Not surprisingly, Tech rejected this notion outright.

Two days before the game, UVa athletic officials notified their counterparts at Tech that the game was off and the guarantee of Tech's expenses was revoked. The Tech team decided to come to

Charlottesville anyway.

The publicity brought out the largest crowd in Lambeth Field history. Both teams took the field shortly after 2 p.m., but UVa officials presented another affidavit for the Tech players to sign; they refused. The standoff persisted right up to the 3 p.m. kickoff time when a compromise was reached and Virginia relented. The affidavit the Tech players had refused to sign was read aloud to the crowd, and the game that wasn't a sure thing got under way.

Football games aren't played on paper. That is, you may attend a Virginia game expecting the Cavaliers to win, but that victory isn't a sure thing. If it were, why bother to go? Any football game worth watching carries with it an element of uncertainty.

Life doesn't get played on paper either, which means that living, too, comes laden with uncertainty. You never know what's going to happen tomorrow or even an hour from now. Oh, sure, you think you know. For instance, right now you may be certain that you'll be at work Monday morning or that you'll have a job next month. Life's uncertainties, though, can intervene at any time and disrupt your nice, pat expectations.

Ironically, while you can't know for sure about this afternoon, you can know for certain about forever. Eternity is a sure thing because it's in God's hands. Your unwavering faith and God's sure promises lock in a certain future for you.

*There is nothing in life so uncertain as a sure thing.*
*-- NHL coach Scotty Bowman*

**Life is unpredictable and tomorrow is uncertain;**
**eternity is a sure thing because God controls it.**

# ON THE MONEY

**Read Luke 16:1-15.**

*"You cannot serve both God and money" (v. 13b).*

Dan Bonner just wanted to be a basketball graduate assistant until, to his surprise, he was offered a head coach's job. He took it -- and lost money in the deal.

In the fall of 1974, Bonner was a senior guard who played well and served as a co-captain for new head coach Terry Holland after two seasons of riding the bench. He knew then that he wanted to coach. When he graduated, he approached athletics director Gene Corrigan about serving as a graduate assistant for the men's team. The job paid $2,500 a year, and Bonner figured that he could pay his graduate-school expenses with the money.

Corrigan had another idea. Barbara Kelly, head coach of the women's team, wanted to step down after leading the program through the first two years of its existence. The AD offered the 22-year-old Bonner the job. He had never considered coaching women before, but he took it. "I think the reason was they just assumed that I knew what I was doing," Bonner said.

Actually, there was more to it than that. Corrigan had plans to make another graduate assistant, Debbie Ryan, who, perhaps coincidentally, was his niece, the head coach. The boss thought, however, that she wasn't ready for the job just yet. "She knew as much about it as I did," Bonner said. "It was kind of silly to have me be the head coach," but that's the way Corrigan wanted it.

# CAVALIERS

Having an assistant coach certainly wasn't all bad for Bonner except perhaps for the way the financial arrangements turned out. Even though he was the head coach, Bonner was still a graduate assistant. So was Ryan. That meant they had to divide the $2,500.

To make it worse, Bonner couldn't get in-state tuition. He ended up getting paid $1,500 and having to pay $1,600 a year for tuition, which wasn't exactly the deal he had in mind.

Having a little too much money at the end of the month may be as bothersome -- if not as worrisome -- as having a little too much month at the end of the money. The investment possibilities are bewildering: stocks, bonds, mutual funds, that group pooling their money to open up a neighborhood coffee shop -- that's a good idea.

You take your money seriously, as well you should. Jesus, too, took money seriously, warning us frequently of its dangers. Money itself is not evil; its peril lies in the ease with which it can usurp God's rightful place as the master of our lives.

Certainly in our age and society, we often measure people by how much money they have. But like our other talents, gifts, and resources, money should primarily be used for God's purposes. God's love must touch not only our hearts but our wallets also.

How much of your wealth are you investing with God?

*Money can buy you everything but happiness. It can pay your fare to everywhere but heaven.*

*-- Pete Maravich*

**Your attitude about money says much
about your attitude toward God.**

# VIRGINIA

## DAY 32

# BAD IDEA

**Read Mark 14:43-50.**

*"The betrayer had arranged a signal with them: 'The one I kiss is the man; arrest him and lead him away under guard'" (v. 44).*

The Pittsburgh Panthers strolled confidently into Scott Stadium for what they expected to be a mismatch. Then the game started, and right off the bat they had a very bad idea.

On Sept. 29, 2007, the Panthers came to town with a defense that was ranked in the top 25 nationally in seven different categories. Facing them was a Cavalier offense that did not exactly strike fear into the Panthers' collective heart.

Allen Billyk, UVa's fifth-year nose tackle, remembered the 2006 opener when Pittsburgh crushed the Cavaliers. "I probably had about 50 people at the game up there, and it left a sour taste in my mouth all year," Billyk said. "I was confident we'd flip the switch, and I was able to get 25 of them to give us another chance."

Billyk's idea was a good one; Pittsburgh's wasn't. The Panthers opened the game by attempting an onside kick. It failed when a Panther touched the ball before it went the required ten yards. No one had yet run a play from scrimmage, and Virginia had the ball at the Pittsburgh 39. As it turned out, the game was over.

The Cavs needed only four plays to put the ball into the end zone on the first of three touchdown passes sophomore quarterback Jameel Sewell would throw -- in the first quarter. The Cavs went on to score four touchdowns before Pitt recorded its initial first down. In the process, UVa scored the game's first 30 points.

When Pitt rallied a little by scoring twice (and by not trying any more onside kicks), Cedric Peerman scored on a 13-yard run and Vic Hall got in from the four. The game was a mismatch, all right. UVa won 44-14, and the rout started when Pitt came up with a perfectly horrendous idea.

That sure-fire investment you made from a pal's hot stock tip. The expensive exercise machine that now traps dust bunnies under your bed. Blond hair. Telling your wife you wanted to eat at the restaurant with the waitresses in little shorts. They seemed like pretty good ideas at the time; they weren't.

We all have bad ideas in our lifetime. They provide some of our most crucial learning experiences.

Some ideas, though, are so irreparably and inherently bad that we cannot help but wonder why they were even conceived in the first place. Almost two thousand years ago a man had just such an idea. Judas' betrayal of Jesus remains to this day one of the most heinous acts of treachery in history.

Turning his back on Jesus was a bad idea for Judas then; it's a bad idea for us now.

*Bat Day seems like a good idea, but I question the advisability of giving bats in the Bronx to 40,000 Yankee fans.*

*– Cartoonist Aaron Bacall*

**We all have some pretty bad ideas
during our lifetimes, but nothing equals the folly
of turning away from Jesus.**

DAY 33

# LIVE ACTION

**Read James 2:14-26.**

*"Faith by itself, if it is not accompanied by action, is dead"*
*(v. 17).*

The Cavs were a missed shot away from suffering a monumental upset, and a whole lot of talking was going down on the floor.

On Dec. 20, 2010, the 7-3 Cavs hosted the Norfolk State Spartans of the Mid-Eastern Athletic Conference, who came into the game at 2-7 and suffering a six-game losing streak. They were not exactly a team everyone figured would waltz into the house of an ACC squad on a four-game winning streak and pull out a victory. That is, not many folks gave them a chance against the Cavs.

So there they were. With only 5.7 seconds left in the game, the Spartans led 49-48. UVa's hopes of avoiding a major embarrassment lay in the hands of freshman K.T. Harrell, who was at the free-throw line with two shots. Earlier in the day, Harrell had been notified he had been selected as the ACC Rookie of the Year for his 20 points in a win over Oregon.

This night, though, he was only 3 of 6 at the foul line, and he proceeded to miss the first shot. That's when some serious talking started.

The Spartan player jockeying at the line to box out Cav center Assane Sene got the conversation started. "Man, he's going to miss it; he's a freshman," he said to Sene. The 7-foot junior from Senegal didn't let that comment pass in silence. "Well, if he misses

# CAVALIERS

it, I'm going to get the offensive rebound or I'm going to tip it," Sene declared.

That certainly merited a response. "Man, you're just talking. You're not going to get it," was the response. Sene's answer was a simple one: "All right, we'll see."

Harrell finally put up his second shot, which abruptly ended all conversation. The attempt rolled off the rim, but Sene was there, his "long arm look[ing] like the old superhero Elastic Man or Stretch Armstrong." Sene reached over everyone -- including his talkative neighbor -- and tipped in the game-winning shot.

Talk is cheap. Consider your neighbor or coworker who talks without saying anything, who makes promises she doesn't keep, who brags about his own exploits, who can always tell you how to do something but never shows up for the work.

How often have you fidgeted through a meeting, impatient to get on with the work everybody is talking about doing? You know -- just as Assane Sene demonstrated against Norfolk State -- that speech without action just doesn't cut it.

That principle applies in the life of a person of faith too. Merely declaring our faith isn't enough, however sincere we may be. It is putting our faith into action that shouts to the world of the depth of our commitment to Christ. Just as Jesus' ministry was a virtual whirlwind of activity, so are we to change the world by doing.

Jesus Christ is alive; so should our faith in Him be.

*Don't talk too much or too soon.*

-- *Bear Bryant*

**Faith that does not reveal itself in action is dead.**

DAY 34

# RUN FOR IT

**Read John 20:1-10.**

*"Peter and the other disciple started for the tomb. Both were running, but the other disciple outran Peter and reached the tomb first" (vv. 3-4).*

Coach Art Guepe had a unique way of holding tryouts for his Virginia football team: The prospects simply lined up and ran.

Guepe coached the Cavaliers from 1946-52. He never had a losing season, and only Al Groh and George Welsh have won more games. His .727 winning percentage (47-17-2) is the best in school history for any coach staying more than two seasons.

Guepe's players considered him a stern taskmaster; they said they knew when it was time for spring practice because Guepe would begin speaking to them. "I was scared to death of Coach Guepe, to be honest with you," said quarterback Gilly Sullivan.

Guepe did his service during World War II at the Iowa Pre-flight School where the service team experimented with a new formation called the split-T. Guepe credited that formation with his success at Virginia. "The other coaches for other teams didn't know anything about the split T," he said.

The defenses were so inept against the split-T that over the course of a game, Guepe would gradually spread his linemen farther and farther apart and the unsuspecting defenses would move with them. "We created our own holes because the stupid defenses would go out with us," recalled end Bob "Rock" Weir.

Guepe's offense thus required speed. According to Dr. John Risher, who played on the 1931 UVa team, Guepe once said that "he didn't care if his recruits could play football as long as they were fast. He could teach them to play football if they were fast."

Guepe's emphasis on speed showed up even during team try-outs. In those days, a coach could put prospects through try-outs before offering them a scholarship. Weir recalled that at the time he was the slowest man on the team, so Guepe would have the prospects race him. If a prospect couldn't beat Weir, "whoop, that kid was gone," Weir said. "They wouldn't look at him."

Hit the ground running -- every morning that's what you do as you leave the house and re-enter the rat race. You run errands; you run though a presentation; you give someone a run for his money; you want to be in the running and never run-of-the-mill.

You're always running toward something, such as your goals, or away from something, such as your past. Many of us spend much of our lives foolhardily attempting to run away from God, the purposes he has for us, and the blessings he seeks to give us.

No matter how hard or how far you run, though, you can never outrun yourself or God. God keeps pace with you, calling you in the short run to take care of the long run by falling to your knees and running for your life -- to Jesus -- just as Peter and the other disciple ran that first Easter morning.

On your knees, you run all the way to glory.

*I never get tired of running. The ball ain't that heavy.*
*-- Herschel Walker*

**You can run to eternity by going to your knees.**

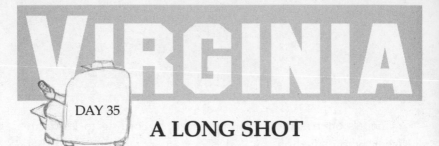

# A LONG SHOT

**Read Matthew 9:9-13.**

*"[Jesus] saw a man named Matthew sitting at the tax collector's booth. 'Follow me,' he told him, and Matthew got up and followed him" (v. 9).*

**F**ew long shots have ever come through as did the Cavaliers in the 1976 ACC Tounament.

"I said we could win but nobody believed me," declared UVa head coach Terry Holland when the tournament was over. He was correct in that nobody believed him, but they had ample reason not to. The Cavs entered the tournament with a 4-8 conference record in the regular season; they were a No. 6 seed. In the tournament's 23 years of hardcourt warfare, Virginia had never won it. Neither had a No. 6 seed. And to win it, the Cavs had to beat three Top-20 teams, each of which had already beaten them twice.

Even the players weren't confident they could pull it off. Before the tournament, some made motel reservations in Fort Lauderdale that conflicted with the NCAA Tournanment. "We'll cancel gladly," said senior forward Wally Walker, the tournament's Most Valuable Player. Holland had no such doubts. "Neither Maryland nor [NC] State is as good as they have been and North Carolina has some weaknesses that can be attacked," he said in reviewing the three teams his long shots would have to beat.

So out they went and handed State its fourth straight loss 75-63 on Thursday and then whipped Maryland 73-65 on Friday. All that got them was a date with 25-2 North Carolina in the finals.

The Cavs used an aggressive man-to-man defense and a deliberate offense to stay close. With only 4:10 to play and the score tied, Carolina went into its four-corners stall. It didn't work. With 34 seconds left, guard Billy Langloh put the Cavs ahead with two free throws. Carolina then turned it over, and center Otis Fulton got a basket on a feed from Langloh. The Cavs won 67-62.

The long shots from UVa were ACC Tournament champions.

Matthew the tax collector was another long shot, an unlikely person to be a confidant of the Son of God. While we may not get all warm and fuzzy about the IRS, our government's revenue agents are nothing like Matthew and his ilk. He bought a franchise, paying the Roman Empire for a license too extort, bully, and steal everything he could from his own people. Tax collectors of the time were "despicable, vile, unprincipled scoundrels."

And yet, Jesus said only two words to this lowlife: "Follow me." Jesus knew that this long shot would make an excellent disciple.

It's the same with us. While we may not be quite as vile as Matthew was, none of us can stand before God with our hands clean and our hearts pure. We are all impossibly long shots to enter God's Heaven. That is, until we do what Matthew did: get up and follow Jesus.

*I don't consider this an upset.*
*-- Terry Holland's recurring statement after each UVa tourney win*

**Only through Jesus does our status change
from being long shots to enter God's Kingdom
to being heavy favorites.**

## DAY 36

# SMART MOVE

**Read 1 Kings 4:29-34; 11:1-6.**

*"[Solomon] was wiser than any other man. . . . As Solomon grew old, his wives turned his heart after other gods, and his heart was not fully devoted to the Lord his God" (vv. 4:31, 11:4).*

The powers that be at Virginia Tech had decided Herman Moore wasn't smart enough to be admitted. Boy, was that a dumb move.

A wide receiver, Moore was first-team All-America in 1990 and finished sixth in the vote for the Heisman Trophy. He set an ACC record in '90 with 1,190 receiving yards and set UVa career records for TD receptions (27) and receiving yards (2,504).

Out of high school, Moore narrowed his choices to Tech and UVa. He had decided for the Hokies until a newspaper article declared Tech wouldn't accept a partial qualifier. That meant Moore who, though he had good grades, had not made the score required on the SAT for freshman eligibility. At the time, Virginia had no policy on partial qualifiers (though the ACC later did adopt Tech's position). The admissions folks reviewed Moore's transcript, decided he would make the score, and accepted him without it. That was good enough for Moore, who signed with UVa and then made the required test score after the signing date.

Throughout his time at Virginia, both Moore and the school were razzed for accepting him. In fact, Moore was an excellent student. A Tech administrator even stepped forward to defend

Moore's academics. "Once [Moore] got the test scores, he had the credentials to be admitted to almost any school that plays Division 1-A football," the administrator said. "It would be an absolute crime to suggest anything else."

Moore graduated from UVa in less than four years, before his football eligibility had expired. For both football and academics, going to Virginia was a smart move for Herman Moore.

Remember that time you wrecked the car when you spilled hot coffee on your lap? That cold morning you fell out of the boat? The time you gave your honey a tool box for her birthday?

Formal education notwithstanding, we all make some dumb moves sometimes because time spent in a classroom is not an accurate gauge of common sense. Folks impressed with their own smarts often grace us with erudite pronouncements that we intuitively recognize as flawed, unworkable, or simply wrong.

A good example is the observation that great intelligence and scholarship are not compatible with faith in God. That is, the more we know, the less we believe. But any incompatibility occurs only because we begin to trust in our own wisdom rather than the wisdom of God. We forget, as Solomon did, that God is the ultimate source of all our knowledge and wisdom and that even our ability to learn is a gift from God.

Not smart at all.

*We're going to live to regret this.*
*-- Frank Beamer to the Tech admissions office about Herman Moore*

**Being truly smart means trusting in God's wisdom rather than only in our own knowledge.**

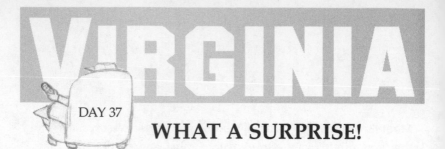

# WHAT A SURPRISE!

### Read 1 Thessalonians 5:1-11.

*"But you, brothers, are not in darkness so that this day should surprise you like a thief" (v. 4).*

The Cavaliers stunned a crowd of 45,100 and a national cable TV audience by racing to a 24-0 lead after less than 20 minutes against one of college football's traditional powers." In other words, UVa surprised the whole country by blasting Texas 37-13.

The win actually was not all that surprising. After all, UVa was ranked 19th and the Horns 13th when they met in Scott Stadium on Sept. 28, 1996. What clearly surprised everyone was that the game was a runaway from the start; Texas never even got close.

"There's not that much difference between the teams," said a diplomatic George Welsh after the rout. "We had everything go our way, and they had nothing go their way."

The Longhorns certainly didn't help themselves, committing six turnovers. But they couldn't do much with Tiki Barber as he pulled off the remarkable feat of scoring on three consecutive runs in the first quarter. After Barber's first score, Ronde Barber's 38-yard interception return set up his brother's second score two plays later. Another two-play drive -- capped by Barber's 12-yard run -- ran the score to 21-0 with 2:35 to go in the first quarter.

Looking for any help for his team, Texas' head coach benched his quarterback, the 1995 Southwest Conference Player of the Year. The backup did manage to pull the Horns to within 24-10 early in

the second half, but they never got any closer.

Quarterback Tim Sherman put the last Cavalier touchdown on the board by faking a pitch to Barber and rambling 24 yards with 13:14 left. That made the score 34-13. "You get to a point where you say to yourself, 'They can't stop us,'" said Tiki Barber.

The Horns couldn't -- and that was a surprise.

Surprise birthday parties are a delight. And what's the fun of opening Christmas presents when we already know what's in them? Some surprises in life provide us with experiences that are both joyful and delightful.

Generally, though, we expend energy and resources to avoid most surprises and the impact they may have upon our lives. We may be surprised by the exact timing of a baby's arrival, but we nevertheless have the bags packed beforehand and the nursery all set for its occupant. Paul used this very image (v. 3) to describe the Day of the Lord, when Jesus will return to claim his own and establish his kingdom. We may be caught by surprise, but we must still be ready.

The consequences of being caught unprepared by a baby's insistence on being born are serious indeed. They pale, however, beside the eternal effects of not being ready when Jesus returns. We prepare ourselves just as Paul told us to (v. 8): We live in faith, hope, and love, ever on the alert for that great, promised day.

*Surprise me.*
                    *-- Yogi Berra on where his wife should have him buried*

**The timing of Jesus' return will be a surprise;
the consequences should not be.**

# VIRGINIA

# IN GOD'S OWN TIME

Read James 5:7-12.

*"Be patient, then, brothers, until the Lord's coming" (v. 7).*

UVa head coach Jeff Jones had just about run out of patience with senior point guard Cory Alexander. The key was "just about" as Jones left him in the game and Alexander led one of the most stirring comebacks in Cavalier basketball history.

On Jan. 14, 1995, about midway through the last half against the Duke Blue Devils, Alexander committed back-to-back turnovers. "I really didn't know what to do," Jones said. "We'd taken him out once already." At the time, Alexander had not scored a point, and Duke was up by 23 at home.

But Jones didn't take Alexander out, and what resulted "may be remembered as the greatest comeback in school history." "I don't know what got into him," Jones said after the game. "Him" was Alexander, who scored 10 points down the stretch and then added 12 more in the game's two overtimes as the Cavs pulled off a stunning 91-88 win. "I'm definitely dumbfounded," said Duke's Jeff Capel after the game. "I couldn't believe it was happening."

But it was. Despite trying Jones' patience, Alexander wound up playing 47 minutes, including 29 of 30 after halftime. He nailed a trey to propel UVa into an 85-82 lead with 1:55 left in the second overtime and then hit a free throw in the closing seconds that pushed UVa's lead back to three.

After his turnovers, Alexander said, he wouldn't have been surprised if Jones had taken him out of the game. "When a coach shows that kind of confidence in you, you've just got to make the best of the situation," Alexander said.

And he certainly did, rewarding Jones' patience by leading a comeback for the ages.

Have you ever left a restaurant because the server didn't take your order quickly enough? Complained at your doctor's office about how long you had to wait? Wondered how much longer a sermon was going to last?

It isn't just the machinations of the world with which we're impatient; we want God to move at our pace, not his. For instance, how often have you prayed and expected – indeed, demanded – an immediate answer from God? And aren't Christians the world over impatient for the glorious day when Jesus will return and set everything right? We're in a hurry but God obviously isn't.

As rare as it seems to be, patience is nevertheless included among the likes of gentleness, humility, kindness, and compassion as attributes of a Christian.

God expects us to be patient. He knows what he's doing, he is in control, and his will shall be done. On his schedule, not ours.

*We decided to stay with him a little bit longer. It's fortunate we did.*
*-- Jeff Jones on being patient enough to keep Cory Alexander in the game in the last half*

**God moves in his own time, so sometimes**
**we just have to wait for him to act,**
**remaining faithful and patient.**

# HOW WE LEAVE

**Read 2 Kings 2:1-12.**

*"A chariot of fire and horses of fire appeared and separated the two of them, and Elijah went up to heaven in a whirlwind" (v. 11).*

**D**on Lawrence was such an old-school gentleman that even as his contract as UVa's head football coach was not renewed, his expressed concern was for his assistant coaches.

Through the 1960s and on into the '70s, the Cavaliers struggled to win on the football field. UVa head coach Bill Elias was honored as the ACC Coach of the Year in 1961, his first season on the job; his record was 4-6. With stars such as quarterback Bob Davis and running back Frank Quayle and innovative offensive guru George Blackburn, Elias' teams were entertaining. For instance, in the '64 season opener, the Cavaliers broke the school and ACC total offense record. They still lost.

But Elias resigned after the '64 season. Blackburn was promoted, and while the offense kept producing points, it didn't produce wins. Blackburn's lone winning season in his six years at the helm came in '68 with a 7-3 record. After the '70 season, athletic director Gene Corrigan decided to replace Blackburn, a move he always regretted. He turned to Lawrence, Blackburn's defensive coordinator.

Concerned because Lawrence was part of a staff with a losing record, the athletic director gave his new coach only a three-year deal. The three seasons weren't successful, netting an 11-22 record, and Lawrence knew the time had come for him to leave.

He exited gracefully, though. He went to Corrigan after his last game and said, "How to you want to work this? Do you want me to resign or do you want to fire me?" Corrigan said Lawrence wasn't particularly concerned about how his release went down; what mattered most was that his assistants were taken care of.

Like Don Lawrence and Elijah, we can't always choose the exact circumstances under which we leave.

You probably haven't always chosen the moves you've made in your life. Perhaps your company transferred you. A landlord didn't renew your lease. An elderly parent needed your care.

Sometimes the only choice we have about leaving is the manner in which we go, whether we depart with style and grace -- as Don Lawrence did -- or not. Our exit from life is the same way. Unless we usurp God's authority over life and death, we can't choose how we die, just how we handle it. Perhaps the most frustrating aspect of dying is that we have at most very little control over the process. As with our birth, our death is in God's hands. We finally must surrender to his will even if we have spent a lifetime refusing to do so.

We do, however, control our destination. How we leave isn't up to us; where we spend eternity is -- and that depends on our relationship with Jesus.

*If I drop dead tomorrow, at least I know I died in good health.*
*-- Former pro football coach Bum Phillips after a physical*

**How you go isn't up to you; where you go is.**

DAY 40

# GIFT-WRAPPED

**Read James 1:12-18.**

*"Every good and perfect gift is from above, coming down from the Father of the heavenly lights" (v. 17).*

Against Miami in 2006, the Cavs got a gift from the officials: a touchdown that should not have been allowed.

The UVa defense held the Hurricanes scoreless for almost 55 minutes on Nov. 18 in taking a 17-7 win at home. On their first possession of the game, the Cavs drove 92 yards with redshirt freshman quarterback Jameel Sewell accounting for all but two of the yards. He completed six of seven passes on the drive and capped it with a 7-yard touchdown run.

While the first touchdown was a pretty routine play, Virginia's second six-pointer marked a first for both head coaches. On the field, the second-quarter score looked a lot like the first TD of the game: Sewell sprinted out and scored from the 2. Despite its obvious success, the play will never be a feature of the Cavalier playbook. That's because Virginia had twelve men on the field.

The coaches caught it just before the snap and were frantically talking back and forth, shouting in panic mode, "Count 'em, count 'em, count 'em." Head coach Al Groh asked over the commotion, "You want a timeout right now?"

But it was too late. Sewell took the snap, and, Groh said, "We all just held our breaths." None of the refs counted the players, and the illegal touchdown was allowed to stand. Instead of facing a

third and goal from the Miami 17, the Cavs had a 13-0 lead.

"I've never been in a game where there was [sic] 12 on the field that wasn't caught," Miami head coach Larry Coker said in a news conference. Groh admitted he hadn't either. "There are a lot of plays that end with 10," he said, "but I can't remember a play when 12 went undetected."

The touchdown was a gift, and the Cavs didn't give it back.

Receiving a gift is nice, but giving has its pleasures too, doesn't it? The children's excitement on Christmas morning. That smile of pure delight on your spouse's face when you came up with a really cool anniversary present. Your dad's surprise that time you didn't give him a tie or socks. There really does seem to be something to this being more blessed to give than to receive.

No matter how generous we may be, though, we are grumbling misers compared to God, who is the greatest gift-giver of all. That's because all the good things in our lives – every one of them – come from God. Friends, love, health, family, the air we breathe, the sun that warms us, even our very lives are all gifts from a profligate God. And here's the kicker: He even gives us eternal life with him through the gift of his son.

What in the world can we possibly give God in return? Our love and our life.

*From what we get, we can make a living; what we give, however, makes a life.*

*– Arthur Ashe*

**Nobody can match God for giving, but you can give him the gift of your love in appreciation.**

# VIRGINIA

# CAN'T GO WRONG

### Read Galatians 6:7-10.

*"Let us not grow weary in doing what is right, for we will reap at harvest time, if we do not give up" (v. 9 NRSV).*

**A**pparently operating on the false assumption that two wrongs make a right, the refs once horrendously botched two calls in quick succession and handed the Cavalier women a bizarre win.

On Dec. 9, 1976, the Cavs and Virginia Tech were tied with less than a minute to play. UVa was bringing the ball up when a ref called a violation for not getting the ball over half court within 10 seconds. Head coach Dan Bonner quite vehemently protested, pointing to the 30-second shot clock, which showed 24 seconds. Unruffled, the ref said she used her own internal counter.

Then both Bonner and his assistant, Debbie Ryan, realized that this flimsy explanation had a very serious flaw: Women's basketball had no 10-second rule. When Bonner pointed this out, the referees appeared quite stunned by the news, huddled, and came up with the original notion of calling for a jump ball.

So far, the officials had been about as wrong about everything as two folks could be. They weren't finished. With a much taller center, Tech easily got the ball, but the Virginia defense knocked it out of bounds with only three seconds left. It looked like overtime as Tech had to go the length of the floor to score, but thanks to yet another wrong call, the Hokies never got the chance.

As Bonner recalled it years later, "The poor girl takes the ball out of bounds. She is standing stock-still, looking around trying to throw it inbounds. And this guy blows his whistle and calls her for traveling."

Bonner didn't care whether it was a makeup call or not. He drew up a play to get the ball in to Barbara Stenzel, who would pass to Kathy Williams, who would drive to the basket. Instead, Stenzel shot and scored.

Nothing about the last minute was right, but UVa had a win.

Doing the right thing is easy when it's little stuff. Giving the quarter back when the cashier gives you too much change, helping a lost child at the mall, or putting a few bucks in the honor box at your favorite fishing hole.

But what about when it costs you? Every day you have multiple chances to do the right thing; in every instance, you have a choice: right or wrong. The factors that weigh into your decisions – including the personal cost to you – reveal much about your character.

Does your doing the right thing ever depend upon your calculation of the odds of getting caught? In the world's eyes, you can't go wrong doing wrong when you won't get caught. That passes for the world's slippery, situational ethics, but it doesn't pass muster with God.

In God's eyes, you can't go wrong doing right. Ever.

*You don't do the right thing once in a while. You do it all the time.*
*-- Vince Lombardi*

**As far as God is concerned,**
**you can never go wrong doing right.**

## DAY 42

# UNBELIEVABLE

**Read Hebrews 3:7-19.**

*"See to it, brothers, that none of you has a sinful, unbelieving heart that turns away from the living God" (v. 12).*

The play was so big and so important that it has been called "the turning point in the Cavaliers' football program." It was also one of the most unbelievable plays in UVa history.

"We've got to beat these guys one of these years." Cavalier head coach George Welsh was the speaker, and "these guys" were the Virginia Tech Hokies. Welsh aimed his words in the general direction of his assistant coaches before the 1984 Tech game. His point was that now was just as good a time as any to whip the intrastate rivals, but the Cavaliers pulled into Blacksburg on Sept. 29 as one-touchdown underdogs.

Tech led early 6-3, but sophomore quarterback Don Majkowski hit freshman wide receiver John Ford with an 18-yard touchdown pass, and Kenny Stadlin ended the half by kicking a school-record 56-yard field goal. UVa led at the break 13-6.

After that, though, the game went Tech's way. With only 10:48 left to play, Tech led 23-13 and Virginia faced a fourth and inches at the Hokie 34. Welsh then made an unbelievable call, and the result was an unbelievable play.

Majkowski faked a dive and let fly with a bomb for a racing Ford. Majkowski later said he thought he had overthrown Ford, but Ford, "listed at 6-3, left his feet around the 5-yard line and was almost horizontal as he gathered the ball in his fingertips." "The way he stretched out and caught that ball, he looked like the Rubber Man," said Tech head coach Bill Dooley.

Ford's unbelievable catch sparked a 26-23 comeback win. The Cavs didn't lose again until the last game of the season.

What we claim not to believe in reveals much about us. UFOs. Global warming. Sasquatch. The designated hitter and aluminum baseball bats.

Most of what passes for our unbelief has little effect on our lives. Does it matter much that we don't believe a Ginsu knife can stay sharp after repeatedly slicing through cans? Or that we're convinced that no team besides Virginia is worth pulling for?

That's not the case, however, when Jesus and God are part of the mix. Quite unbelievably, we often hear people blithely assert they don't believe in God. Or brazenly declare they believe in God but don't believe Jesus was anything but a good man and a great teacher.

At this point, unbelief becomes dangerous because God doesn't fool around with scoffers. He locks them out of the Promised Land, which isn't a country in the Middle East but Heaven itself.

Given that scenario, it's downright unbelievable that anyone would not believe.

*I shall never forget it. It was unbelievable, just an unbelievable catch.*
*-- Tech coach Bill Dooley on John Ford's catch*

**Perhaps nothing is as unbelievable as that some people insist on not believing in God or his son.**

DAY 43

# WHO, ME?

**Read Judges 6:11-23.**

*"'But Lord,' Gideon asked, 'how can I save Israel? My clan is the weakest in Manasseh, and I am the least in my family'" (v. 15).*

I was like, 'I did that.'" Jason Rogers' sense of wonder at his dunk off a fast break was nothing compared to that of his coach and the fans over the game he played against mighty Maryland.

Rogers was one of those courtesy starters on senior night when UVa hosted the 8th-ranked and defending national champion Maryland Terrapins on March 10, 2003. It was the first start of his career, one of those honors in which the senior maybe plays until the first TV time out. After all, Rogers had played a total of 14 minutes in nine games all season.

Rogers didn't play like a courtesy starter, though, as much to his surprise as everybody else's. Less than two minutes into the game, he blocked a shot, then hit a jump hook on the trip down the floor. "When I threw that jump hook," he said, "I was like, 'Dear God, just hit the rim.' That was one of the ugliest things that's ever come off my hands."

When Rogers got his first break with 12:05 left in the half, he had five points, four rebounds, and three blocked shots. Sensing something special was happening, the crowd began to repeatedly chant his name. At no time, though, did he excite everyone more than with 4:30 left in the first half when he banged home a dunk on a fast break. The old cliche is he brought the house down, and that's exactly what Rogers did. "It brought everything down for me," he said. "I was like, 'I did that.'"

For the night, the courtesy starter had 12 points, six rebounds, three assists, and several blocks. The Cavs pulled off the upset 80-78 in overtime.

"I couldn't believe it," said head coach Pete Gillen of Rogers' "Who, me?" night. "I was stunned." So was Maryland.

Like Jason Rogers, you've probably experienced your personal "Who, me?" moment, though perhaps it wasn't as pleasant as his was. How about that time the teacher called on you when you hadn't done a lick of homework? Or when the hypnotist pulled you out of a room full of folks to be his guinea pig? You've had the wide-eyed look and the turmoil in your midsection when you were suddenly singled out and found yourself in a situation you neither sought nor were prepared for.

You may feel exactly as Gideon did about being called to serve God in some way, quailing at the very notion of being audacious enough to teach Sunday school, lead a small group study, or coordinate a high school prayer club. Who, me? Hey, who's worthy enough to do anything like that?

The truth is that nobody is – but that doesn't seem to matter to God. And it's his opinion, not yours, that counts.

*That's the best he's played in four years.*
*-- Coach Pete Gillen on Jason Rogers' game against Maryland*

**You're right in that no one is worthy to serve God,**
**but the problem is that doesn't matter to God.**

# VIRGINIA

## DAY 44

## I CAN'T STAND IT!

### Read Exodus 32:1-20.

*"[Moses'] anger burned and he threw the tablets out of his hands, breaking them to pieces at the foot of the mountain" (v. 19).*

**V**irginia managed to win by her usual slugging." That infantile comment from a Norfolk newspaper in 1901 reflected the frustration VPI's fans felt as year after year the Cavs pounded them.

The UVa-Tech football rivalry began in 1895 with a game that "was an embarrassment for the Hokies." Virginia blasted them 38-0. That was bad enough, but 1896 was worse: The Wahoos won 44-0. On the field, the Hokies were already letting their frustration show. The UVa student newspaper said that the visitors "at times showed an unnecessary degree of roughness" but -- with a bit of smugness -- attributed the behavior to "their disappointment in finding themselves unable to hold the score down."

Virginia won with another shutout in 1899 before Tech at least scored in a 17-5 loss in 1900. After the game, the Hokie manager wired back to Blacksburg that VPI had been robbed. This was certainly sour grapes, since UVa had simply run over the Hokies 395 yards to 145. Never missing a chance to rub it in, the UVa student paper responded, "We were sorry to learn that VPI considered herself badly treated in the game." The writer apologized for UVa's inability to find officials that would satisfy the Hokies and commiserated with the losers for always being "so down on your luck here" in Charlottesville.

After a 16-0 UVa win in 1901, VPI's frustration must have reached its zenith in the 1902 game, which even the Cavalier newspaper admitted was won by an illegal touchdown. Captain Walter "Down Home" Council ran for 23 yards for the game's only score on a play that evidently should have been blown dead.

The traffic light catches you when you're running late for work or a doctor's appointment. The bureaucrat gives you red tape when you want assistance. Your daughter refuses to take her homework seriously. Makes your blood boil, doesn't it? Like VPI in its early games against Virginia, we know frustration first-hand.

Frustration is part of God's testing ground that is life, even if much of what frustrates us today results from man-made organizations, bureaucracies, and machines. What's important is not that you encounter frustration—that's a given—but how you handle it. Do you respond with curses, screams, and violence? Or with a deep breath, a silent prayer, and calm persistence, and patience?

It may be difficult to imagine Jesus stuck in traffic or waiting for hours in a long line in a government office. It is not difficult, however, to imagine how he would act in such situations, and, thus, to know exactly how you should respond. No matter how frustrated you are.

*The VPI team gave an exhibition of puerile behavior at every decision of the umpire.*
*-- The Virginia student newspaper on the 1900 game*

**Frustration is indeed a vexing part of life,**
**but God expects us to handle it gracefully.**

DAY 45

# MIDDLE OF NOWHERE

**Read Genesis 28:10-22.**

*"When Jacob awoke from his sleep, he thought, 'Surely the Lord is in this place, and I was not aware of it'" (v. 16).*

Just down the road from Red Ash and Raven. A couple of turns away from Mavisdale and Rowe. Be careful, you might miss it right there in the middle of nowhere -- the community where UVa found the tight end who rewrote the school's record book.

Actually, what Virginia originally found in Swords Creek, Va., was a quarterback. Heath Miller was the signal caller for Honaker High School; he had to go down the road to school for a simple reason: That's where the high school was. The move didn't quite classify as a leap into the big-time. At least until a few years ago, Honaker didn't have a stoplight -- but neither did Swords Creek. "There's an elementary school and a post office," said Miller's mother, "but no major businesses and definitely not a stoplight."

But what Honaker did have in the 2000 football season was Miller, who set several school passing records and led the school to its first-ever state championship game. Honaker played in Group A, which some years doesn't send a single player to major colleges on a football scholarship. But no matter where he played his high-school football, Miller was hard to miss. He stood 6-foot-5, weighed 225 pounds, and was the Group A football player of the year in 2000. The big-time beckoned and Miller answered.

The move that launched him into the big-time came in the fall of 2001 when Miller willingly shifted to tight end. His teammates dubbed him "Big Money" for his ability to gain first downs and score touchdowns. He started at UVa for three seasons (2002-04) and led the team in receiving each year. He left UVa holding ACC records for most career receptions, yards, and touchdowns by a tight end. In 2004, he was a unanimous All-America.

After hitting the big-time at Virginia, Miller went on to an even bigger stage as an All-Pro tight end for the Pittsburgh Steelers.

Ever had lunch in Five Forks? Or had a cup of coffee in Java? Crooned in Singers Glen? Visited Motley? Or Mascot?

They are among the many small communities, some of them nothing more than crossroads, that dot the Virginia countryside. Not on any interstate highway, they seem to be in the middle of nowhere, the type of place where Heath Miller could be found relaxing at home. They're just hamlets we zip through on our way to somewhere important.

But don't be misled; those villages are indeed special and wonderful. That's because God is in Kenbridge and Skipwith just as he is in Richmond, Roanoke, and Charlottesville. Even when you are far off the roads well traveled, you are with God. As Jacob discovered one rather astounding morning, the middle of nowhere is, in fact, holy ground -- because God is there.

*The middle of nowhere is the place that teaches you that crossing the goal line first is not as important as the course you took to get there.*
*— Dive instructor Ridlon Kiphart*

**No matter how far off the beaten path you travel,
you are still on holy ground because God is there.**

DAY 46

# MEMORY LOSS

### Read 1 Corinthians 11:17-29.

*"[D]o this in remembrance of me" (v. 24).*

**A**nthony Oliver remembered -- and helped UVa to a big win.

Oliver was a four-year letterman from 1989-92 and a team captain for the Cavaliers. As a sophomore, he kept a reminder of an incident from his freshman season that served to inspire him.

On Jan. 25, 1989, the Cavs' starting guard tandem of Richard Morgan (28 points) and John Crotty (21 points) led the team to a thrilling 113-106 overtime win over Virginia Tech. Oliver didn't play much or well in the game as a freshman guard off the bench. He played only six minutes, scored only two points, and had four turnovers. "I was having a tough time," he admitted.

At one point, soon after Oliver went into the game, Tech's high-scoring star Bimbo Coles stole the ball from him and went in for a layup. As Oliver remembered it, "We were standing at midcourt and [Coles] started talking. I didn't say anything. There was nothing I could say."

And what was it Coles said to him that led Oliver to write it down on a slip of paper, carry that paper with him for a year, and then pull that slip out the night before the Tech game and stare at it? "He told me I didn't belong at this level," Oliver said.

Oliver had to wait until Jan. 24, 1990, to prove himself. When the night finally came, he was ready. "I was really pumped up for this one," Oliver said. Sure enough, it was one shooting guard on

another; he was assigned to guard Coles all night.

And just how did it turn out? Quite well. Oliver both outshot and outscored Coles as long as the game was in doubt. The Cavs took command with a 13-0 run in the last half and won easily 77-59. Coles hit only 6 of 20 shots; Oliver held him to 12 points, though Coles added 8 points in the last three minutes when it didn't matter. Oliver hit 6 of 11 shots and scored 13 points.

Anthony Oliver remembered -- and the memory inspired him.

Memory makes us who we are. Whether our memories are dreams or nightmares, they shape us and to a large extent determine both our actions and our reactions. Alzheimer's is so terrifying because it steals our memory from us, and in the process we lose ourselves. We disappear.

The greatest tragedy of our lives is that God remembers. In response to that memory, he condemns us for our sin. On the other hand, the greatest joy of our lives is that God remembers. In response to that memory, he came as Jesus to wash even the memory of our sins away.

Through memory, we encounter revival. At the Last Supper, Jesus instructed his disciples and us to remember. In sharing this unique meal with fellow believers and remembering Jesus and his actions, we meet Christ again, not just as a memory but as an actual living presence. To remember is to keep our faith alive.

*When he says something like that, it sticks with you.*
*-- Anthony Oliver on Bimbo Coles' insult*

**We remember Jesus, and God**
**will not remember our sins.**

# VIRGINIA

DAY 47

# CHEAP TRICKS

**Read Acts 19:11-20.**

*"The evil spirit answered them, 'Jesus I know, and I know about Paul, but who are you?'" (v. 15)*

Without the element of surprise, a trick play will not work in a football game. Yet, the Cavs once used the same trick play twice in a row to upset Georgia Tech in the closing seconds.

On No. 10, 2001, Al Groh's first Cav team was a 14-point underdog to the 20th-ranked Yellow Jackets. The game turned out to be one of the most exciting contests in Scott Stadium history. UVa fell behind by 13 in the first half, rallied, and then gave up the lead three times in the fourth quarter. Incredibly, the Jackets and the Cavs scored seven touchdowns in the last period.

With 9:24 left in the game, Georgia Tech scored to take a 26-21 lead. It lasted only 17 seconds, the time it took Tavon Mason, who had caught a 19-yard scoring pass in the first half, to return the kickoff 100 yards, the longest in UVa history.

Tech eventually took a 38-33 lead with only 1:45 left, but once again the Cavs had an answer. Virginia quickly moved to its own 49. With time running out, offensive coordinator Bill Musgrave decided to pull a trick play out of his bag; he called for the "hook and lateral," a short pass with a pitch to a trailing player.

UVa Quarterback Bryson Spinner, who threw five touchdown passes in the game, hit Billy McMullen with a 14-yard completion -- and that was it. Because of the defense, McMullen decided not to

risk pitching the ball to freshman Alvin Pearman, trailing on the play. Pearman later called McMullen's decision "a smart play."

But then Spinner pulled a little trickery of his own. He hustled the offense to the line of scrimmage and shouted out, "Same play, same play." This time when he hit McMullen, three confident Tech defenders converged on the receiver, leaving Pearman open. McMullen lateraled the ball and Pearman went the distance with only 22 seconds left for the 39-38 win.

Scam artists are everywhere — and they love trick plays. An e-mail encourages you to send money to some foreign country to get rich. That guy at your front door offers to resurface your driveway at a ridiculously low price. A TV ad promises a pill to help you lose weight without diet or exercise.

You've been around; you check things out before deciding. The same approach is necessary with spiritual matters, too, because false religions and bogus Christian denominations abound. The key is what any group does with Jesus. Is he the son of God, the ruler of the universe, and the only way to salvation? If not, then what the group espouses is something other than the true Word of God.

The good news about Jesus does indeed sound too good to be true. But the only catch is that there is no catch. No trick -- just the truth.

*Desperate times call for desperate measures.*
*-- Al Groh on the trick play that beat Georgia Tech*

**God's promises through Jesus sound too good to**
**be true, but the only catch is that there is no catch.**

# GOOD SPORTS

### Read Titus 2:1-8.

*"Show integrity, seriousness and soundness of speech that
cannot be condemned, so that those who oppose you may
be ashamed because they have nothing bad to say about
us" (vv. 7b, 8).*

**B**ill Dudley, one of UVa's greatest players ever (See Devotion
No. 90.), once displayed such sportsmanship in high school that
his coach was furious -- but it eventually led to a win.

Dudley is such a legend that even though he last played pro
ball in 1953, he was a free agent in the video game Madden NFL
08. He is a member of the college and pro halls of fame and the
Virginia Sports Hall of Fame.

In addition to being one of the greatest football players in the
history of the game, Dudley was a consummate sportsman. In
high school, he once played a game on a field that was cut out of a
mountainside and had a seeping spring on the six-yard line. His
coach and he agreed that he should aim his punts at the puddle
to make a fumble more likely.

Dudley did just that, landing a punt dead center in the puddle.
The officials ruled the ball dead; the other team would have to
snap the ball from the water. But Dudley exercised his role as the
team captain and allowed the ref to move the ball out of the water
to the center of the field. His infuriated coach kept muttering on
the sideline, "At the half, I want to get ahold of Dudley."

Just before the half, though, the other squad fumbled in the middle of the puddle and Dudley's team recovered. The referees huddled and decided to reciprocate Dudley's original act of sportsmanship. They moved the ball to the center of the field, out of the water, and Dudley scored what turned out to be the game-winning touchdown easily from there.

One of life's paradoxes is that many who would never consider cheating on the tennis court or the racquetball court to gain an advantage think nothing of doing so in other areas of their life. In other words, the good sportsmanship they practice on the golf course or even on the Monopoly board doesn't carry over. They play with the truth, cut corners, abuse others verbally, run roughshod over the weak and the helpless, and generally cheat whenever they can to gain an advantage on the job or in their personal relationships.

But good sportsmanship is a way of living, not just of playing. Shouldn't you accept defeat without complaint (You don't have to like it.); win gracefully without gloating; treat your competition with fairness, courtesy, generosity, and respect? That's the way one team treats another in the name of sportsmanship. That's the way one person treats another in the name of Jesus.

*Now what are you going to say to Dudley?*
*-- Assistant coach to the head coach when Dudley scored easily*
*after the refs moved the ball out of the water*

**Sportsmanship -- treating others with courtesy,**
**fairness, and respect -- is a way of living,**
**not just a way of playing.**

DAY 49

# DREAM WORLD

**Read Joshua 3.**

*"All Israel passed by until the whole nation had completed the crossing on dry ground" (v. 17b).*

It's exactly the kind of thing an unwitting, rather naive college freshman might say to his equally callow contemporaries. Only in this case, the dream came true.

One September evening in 1991, A.J. Wood, a freshman forward on the Virginia soccer team, casually suggested to the rookie teammates walking with him that they ought to think big. Real big. Four-straight-NCAA-championships big. "That's what we set our sights on," Wood said, apparently with a straight but guileless face. But then so a listener wouldn't think him a total dork, he added, "We didn't expect it to come true."

In all honesty, it was a pretty dubious idea, yet on Dec. 11, 1994, in Davidson, N.C., senior Wood and his teammates took the field with a shot at realizing their far-fetched dream. Only the Hoosiers of Indiana stood between them and their fourth straight national championship.

"We're like regulars here," Wood said, referring to Davidson. "We've outlasted some restaurants." As evidence, he pointed out that the team's favorite eating place was now a steak house. "Last year it was an Italian place. The year before, a sandwich shop." Indiana's head coach agreed with Wood's observation, saying Virginia was at the NCAAs so much the team should rent a condo.

# CAVALIERS

The top-ranked Hoosiers were the favorites to end the dream, but Wood -- he who had first voiced the whole ridiculous notion -- scored in the 21st minute of the first half. After that, the aggressive Cavalier defense took over and Virginia won 1-0.

The four seniors left on the team from that evening four years before had achieved their dream: four championship rings.

No matter how tightly or doggedly we cling to our dreams, devotion to them won't make them a reality. Moreover, the cold truth is that all too often dreams don't come true even when we put forth a mighty effort. The realization of dreams generally results from a head-on collision of persistence, timing, and luck.

But what if our dreams don't come true because they're not the same dreams God has for us? That is, they're not good enough and, in many cases, they're not big enough.

God calls us to great achievements because God's dreams for us are greater than our dreams for ourselves. Could the Israelites, wallowing in the misery of slavery, even dream of a land of their own? Could they imagine actually going to such a place?

The fulfillment of such great dreams occurs only when our dreams and God's will for our lives are the same. Our dreams should be worthy of our best – and worthy of God's involvement in making them come true.

*An athlete cannot run with money in his pocket. He must run with hope in his heart and dreams in his head.*
*-- Olympic Gold Medalist Emil Zatopek*

**If our dreams are to come true, they must be worthy of God's involvement in them.**

# VIRGINIA

### DAY 50

# A ROARING SUCCESS

### Read Galatians 5:16-26.

*"So I say, live by the Spirit. . . . The sinful nature desires what is contrary to the Spirit. . . . The acts of the sinful nature are obvious: . . . I warn you, as I did before, that those who live like this will not inherit the kingdom of God" (vv. 16, 17, 19, 21).*

All college football programs have down periods at some time in their history. A number of reasons may account for this, but UVa once had "a period of losing and mediocrity" brought about by a most unusual cause: the Cavaliers' success on the field.

With the arrival of head coach Art Guepe and a number of veterans returning from the war, Charlottesville blossomed into a college football hotbed after World War II. Guepe never had a losing year, and his last three Cavalier teams (1950-52) were 8-1, 8-2, and 8-2.

Not everyone in the community, however, was happy with what was perceived as an overemphasis on football. Gilly Sullivan, who played quarterback for Guepe, observed, "It appeared to me that the administration of the University itself wasn't all that excited about a successful athletic program."

In 1951, the university commissioned a committee to study the role of athletics at UVa. The group concluded "that the school had gotten caught up in 'big-time athletics'" and called for "a deemphasis of sports, particularly football."

# CAVALIERS

When the administration allowed Guepe to leave for Vanderbilt after the 1952 season, "Saturday afternoons in Charlottesville became bitter, frustrating affairs." Beginning in 1953, only twice in the next thirty years would the Cavs win more than they lost, the program done in by its own success.

Are you a successful person? Your answer, of course, depends upon how you define success. Is the measure of your success based on the number of digits in your bank balance, the square footage of your house, that title on your office door, the size of your boat?

Certainly the world determines success by wealth, fame, prestige, awards, and possessions. Our culture screams that life is all about gratifying your own needs and wants. If it feels good, do it. It's basically the Beach Boys' philosophy of life.

But all success of this type has one glaring shortcoming: You can't take it with you. Eventually, Daddy takes the T-bird away. Like life itself, all these things are fleeting.

A more lasting way to approach success is through the spiritual rather than the physical. The goal becomes not money or backslaps by sycophants but eternal life spent with God. Success of that kind is forever.

*There was a time when we didn't even have to worry about scouting them.*
*-- UVa player and coach Evan J. Male on the Cavs' success against VPI in the 1940s and early '50s*

**Success isn't permanent, and failure isn't fatal --**
**unless you're talking about**
**your relationship with God.**

## DAY 51

# THE GOOD FIGHT

**Read 1 Corinthians 10:1-6.**

*"Though we live in the world, we do not wage war as the world does. The weapons we fight with are not the weapons of the world" (vv. 3-4a).*

**S**he "must have been about 75 years old," but she wanted to fight the UVa ticket manager in one of the biggest game-day fiascoes in school history.

Virginia's practice in the late 1970s was to make duplicate sets of the tickets sent to opponents for home football games. This allowed the school to make tickets available to Cavalier fans if the school didn't use its allotment. Ticket manager Dennis Womack, who was the head baseball coach for 23 seasons (1981-2003), knew that Virginia Tech fans would buy all their tickets for the 1978 game, so the spare set was locked in a vault in the ticket office.

"Somehow, over the course of the fall," Womack recalled, "the tickets mysteriously got sold. . . . Come game day, everybody's out in the parking lot socializing until about 20 minutes before kickoff. . . . All of a sudden, we've got people looking at each other and realizing they've got the same seats."

The game was sold out; Womack couldn't secure hundreds of extra tickets. He went to the section with the counterfeiting problem to find a bunch of very angry folks. He tried talking to them, but one Tech fan, who, Womack said, "must have been 75 years old . . . wanted to fight me." The feisty senior citizen "was calling me some names and told me, if I came off that platform [on which Womack was standing to address the crowd], she was going to whup me. Of course, I wasn't about to come down."

Womack managed to avoid a fight that he could only lose and get his hands on a few extra tickets. He also allowed some folks to sit on a hill. Others, though, just got mad and left. Many of the disgruntled Tech fans later called Womack and demanded their money back; not the Cav fans, though. UVa won 17-7.

Violence is not the Christian way, but what about confrontation? Following Jesus' admonition to turn the other cheek has rendered many a Christian meek and mild in the name of obedience. But we need to remember that the Lord we follow once bullwhipped a bunch of folks who turned God's temple into a flea market.

With Christianity in America under attack as never before, we must stand up for and fight for our faith. Who else is there to stand up for Jesus if not you? Our pretty little planet -- including our nation -- is a battleground between good and evil. We are far from helpless in this fight because God has provided us with a powerful set of weapons. Prayer, faith, hope, love, the Word of God itself and the Holy Spirit -- these are the weapons at our command with which to vanquish evil and godlessness.

We are called by God to use them, to fight the good fight, not just in our own lives but in our nation and in our world.

*It was a real mess.*
*-- Dennis Womack on the ticket fiasco of 1978*

**'Stand Up, Stand Up for Jesus' is not an antiquated hymn but a contemporary call to fight for our Lord.**

### DAY 52

# GOOD LUCK

### Read 1 Samuel 28:3-20.

*"Saul then said to his attendants, 'Find me a woman who is a medium, so I may go and inquire of her'" (v. 7).*

From Mohawk haircuts to the way a coach raked the mound in the bullpen, the Cavaliers of 2010 followed a time-honored baseball tradition of being superstitious.

On his way to a plane, junior pitcher and closer Kevin Arico always let his glove pass through the X-ray machine. He never took the chance of checking his glove with his luggage.

Virginia assistant coach Karl Kuhn was always careful to rake the mound in the Cavalier bullpen exactly the same way.

Greg Parker, the father of center fielder Jarrett Parker, always walked through the stadiums each time his son was at the plate, always hoping to find the exact spot that would translate into a hit. It may have helped. An All-America, Parker set school season records for runs, hits, and total bases in 2009. In 2010, he played the entire season without making an error.

Some of the Cavs were quite superstitious about their haircuts. In 1009, All-ACC second baseman Phil Gosselin began the season 0-for-16. He sought to break out of his slump with a Mohawk from catcher Franco Valdes. When Gosselin opened up the 2010 season hot and kept hitting, he took the opposite approach: He went the whole season without a haircut. Other players -- including Steven Proscia, Valdes himself, Rob Amaro, Ryan Levine, and Stephen

# CAVALIERS

Bruno -- followed the Gosselin example in 2010 of getting radical haircuts to break hitting slumps.

Talent had much more to do with it than superstition, but something worked for the 2010 team. The Cavaliers set a school record with 51 wins and won both the ACC's Coastal Division and the regional they hosted.

Black cats are right pretty. A medium is a steak. A key chain with a rabbit's foot wasn't too lucky for the rabbit. And what in the world is a blarney stone? About as superstitious as you get is to say "God bless you" when somebody sneezes.

You look indulgently upon good-luck charms, tarot cards, astrology, palm readers, and the like; they're really just amusing and harmless. So what's the problem? Nothing, as long as you conduct yourself with the belief that superstitious objects and rituals – from broken mirrors to your daily horoscope – can't bring about good or bad luck. You aren't willing to let such notions and nonsense rule your life.

The danger of superstition lies in its ability to lure you into trusting it, thus allowing it some degree of influence over your life. In that case, it subverts God's rightful place.

Whether or not it's superstition, something does rule your life. It should be God – and God alone.

*Everybody has their own little quirks in this sport and [not cutting my hair] is mine this year. That's baseball for you.*
-- *Phil Gosselin*

**Superstitions may not rule your life, but
something does; it should be God and God alone.**

DAY 53

# DECIDE FOR YOURSELF

**Read John 6:60-69.**

*"The words I have spoken to you are spirit and they are life. Yet there are some of you who do not believe" (vv. 63b-64a).*

In the last game of his stellar career, Cavalier halfback Frank Quayle made an unusual decision. One of UVa's most notable records was his for the smashing, but he refused to take it.

Quayle is one of Virginia's greatest football players, the backbone of the 1968 Cavalier team that finished 7-3 and broke the program's long losing skid. He led the ACC in all-purpose yards all three seasons that he played (1966-68). As a senior, he was the league's Player of the Year; UVa retired his number 24.

Quayle's first two seasons were very good, "but he achieved greatness his last go-around in 1968." As the season wore on, it became apparent that either Quayle or Clemson's Buddy Gore would finish the season as the ACC's career rushing leader. "Frank never talked about it, but we did," said quarterback Gene Arnette. "We wanted the record for him."

Late in the season, injuries sidelined Gore while Quayle kept running and the Cavs kept winning. He finished his career in spectacular fashion against Maryland. His third touchdown of the game put the Cavs up 28-23 with four minutes left to play. When the defense held, Virginia had only to run out the clock.

At that point, Quayle had 216 yards on 29 carries. His 1,213

# CAVALIERS

yards were a new ACC single-season rushing record, and his career total of 2,695 yards had left Gore far behind in the race for the career rushing record. But as Virginia got the ball one last time, Quayle stood one yard shy of John Papit's 1949 school rushing record. He decided not to go for it. "For some reason," he said, "I just didn't want the school record. It seemed like too much."

As with Frank Quayle's selfless choice, the decisions you have made along the way have shaped your life at each pivotal moment. Some decisions you made suddenly and carelessly; some you made carefully and deliberately; some were forced upon you. Surprisingly, some of those spur-of-the-moment decisions have turned out better than your carefully considered ones.

Of all your life's decisions, however, none is more important than one you cannot ignore: What have you done with Jesus? Even in his time, people chose to follow Jesus or to reject him, and nothing has changed; the decision must still be made and nobody can make it for you. Ignoring Jesus won't work either; that is, in fact, a decision, and neither he nor the consequences of your decision will go away.

Carefully considered or spontaneous – how you arrive at a decision for Jesus doesn't matter; all that matters is that you get there.

*If you make a decision that you think is the proper one at the time, then that's the correct decision.*

-- *John Wooden*

**A decision for Jesus may be spontaneous or considered; what counts is that you make it.**

DAY 54

# CELEBRATION TIME

**Read Exodus 14:26-31; 15:19-21.**

*"Miriam the prophetess, Aaron's sister, took a tambourine in her hand, and all the women followed her, with tambourines and dancing" (v. 15:20).*

Excited Georgia fans swarmed onto the field and started doing the "snake dance" to celebrate a win over Virginia. Their celebration turned out to be a mite premature.

The Cavalier football team of 1915 was a powerhouse, finishing 8-1 and becoming the first team from the South to defeat Yale. (See devotion No. 75.) While they outscored their opponents 219-26 that season, the Cavs needed one of the most bizarre finishes in school history to beat Georgia.

Star UVa halfback Eugene "Buck" Mayer, the first player from a Southern school to be named first-team All-America, broke loose around an end for a touchdown. When the Cavs missed the extra point, though, Georgia had a 7-6 lead as time wound down.

The Cavaliers were at the Georgia 15 when a whistle blew that apparently ended the game. Bulldog fans, exuberant about what was a monumental win over what many considered the best team in the South, took to the field and formed up for a "snake dance," which was a custom of the time to celebrate wins.

But the field judge announced, to the fans' great trepidation, that eight seconds remained on the clock. Virginia had time for one last play. Or two, as it turned out. Mayer ran a sweep to the sideline and managed to get out of bounds. With the clock stopped, R.E. Tippett stood at the Georgia 20 and drop-kicked a field goal. Georgia protested that the kick was wide, but the officials ruled it was good.

The field judge promptly blew his whistle and announced that this time the game was truly over. Virginia had a 9-7 win, leaving the once-celebrating Georgia fans stunned and starting a celebration by the ecstatic UVa contingent.

You know what it takes to throw a good party. You start with your closest friends, add some salsa and chips, fire up the grill and throw on some burgers and dogs, and then top it all off with the Cavalier game on TV.

You probably also know that any old excuse will do to get people together for a celebration. All you really need is a sense that life is pretty good right now.

That's the thing about having Jesus as part of your life· He turns every day into a celebration of the good life. No matter what tragedies or setbacks life may have in store, the heart given to Jesus will find the joy in living. That's because such a life is spent with quiet confidence in God's promise of salvation through Jesus, a confidence that inevitably bubbles up into a joy the troubles of the world cannot touch.

When a life is celebrated with Jesus, the party never stops.

*Aim high and celebrate that!*
— *Marathon runner Bill Rodgers*

**With Jesus, life is one big party because it becomes a celebration of victory and joy.**

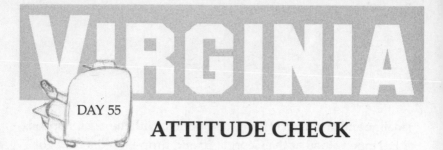

# ATTITUDE CHECK

### Read 1 Thessalonians 5:12-22.

*"Give thanks in all circumstances, for this is God's will
for you in Christ Jesus" (v. 18).*

**W**hen you pretty much know that you're the greatest team in
school history to that point, it's kind of tough to avoid developing
an attitude. But head coach Debbie Ryan had "the tape."

The Cavalier women's basketball team of 1989-90 set a school
record for wins (subsequently broken by both the 1990-91 and
the 1991-92 squads) with a 29-6 record. They were the ACC
Tournament champions -- and they were indeed very, very good.

Ryan knew right off that the team had a chance to be something special. After all, she had two All-Americas in guards Dawn
Staley (See Devotion No. 19.) and Tammi Reiss, an honorable
mention All-America in Tonya Cardoza, and two future pro
players in Heidi and Heather Burge.

So at the first team meeting in 1989, Ryan made sure this
very talented bunch went into the season with an attitude that
included a healthy dose of humility. She showed them a tape of
UVa's game against Tennessee in the NCAA regionals the season
before. Tennessee had won by 33 points. She told her team, "Any-
time we're feeling a little too good about ourselves, I think I'm
going to pop this tape in here."

Sure enough, when the Cavs made it to the Elite Eight with a
win over Providence, Tennessee was waiting for them. "As soon

# CAVALIERS

as the pairings came out, I think people thought Tennessee would win the region in a cakewalk," Ryan said. They would surely beat the second-seeded Cavs for the fourth year in a row.

But Ryan's team had the right attitude: They weren't too sure of themselves *and* they weren't intimidated. Behind Staley's 25 points and junior forward Tekshia Ward's 19 points and 11 rebounds, they went out and beat Tennessee 79-75 in overtime to earn the program's first-ever trip to the Final Four.

How's your attitude? You can fuss because your house is not as big as some, because a coworker talks too much, or because you have to take pills every day. Or you can appreciate your home for providing warmth and shelter, the co-worker for the lively conversation, and the medicine for keeping you reasonably healthy.

Whether life is endured or enjoyed depends largely on your attitude. An attitude of thankfulness to God offers you the best chance to get the most out of your life because living in gratitude means you choose joy in your life no matter what your circumstances. This world does not exist to satisfy you, so chances are it will not. True contentment and joy are found in a deep, abiding relationship with God, and the proper way to approach God is not with haughtiness or anger but with gratitude for all he has given you.

*I never had to show [that tape] again.*
> *-- Debbie Ryan on the attitude of the 1989-90 team*

**Your attitude goes a long way
toward determining the quality of your life
and your relationship with God.**

## DAY 56

# GOOD TIMES

**Read Psalm 30.**

*"You turned my wailing into dancing; you removed my sackcloth and clothed me with joy" (v. 11).*

As weeks go, Brandon Woods had a pretty good one.

On Oct. 3, 2009, the senior defensive back made only his fourth career start, stepping in for injured safety Rodney McLeod against the heavily favored North Carolina Tar Heels. Woods had arrived at UVa as a highly rated wide receiver, but he was soon moved over to defense and often wondered what would have happened had he stayed on offense. He even told head coach Al Groh that he was available if they needed him at wide receiver.

He was needed on defense against UNC, and he was a part of an overwhelming defensive performance. The underdog Cavs simply pushed the Tar Heels around in a 16-3 upset. The defense limited Carolina to only 39 yards rushing and nine first downs and even set the table for the game-clinching score. End Nate Collins pressured UNC's quarterback and deflected a pass that cornerback Chase Minnifield picked off. That set up Mikell Simpson's 8-yard touchdown run that put the final score on the board with 5:49 to play.

And with fifteen family members and friends looking on, Brandon Woods was a part of it all. But his surprise start and good play were probably not the highlight of his week -- or at least he probably should never say out loud that it was so. Only the Satur-

# CAVALIERS

day before, during an off week, he married his longtime sweet-heart, becoming the Cavs' first married player since Jon Copper in 2008. Woods' new wife, Khama, had no problem with holding the wedding in the middle of the season. "I knew it would make him play better," she said.

Even during a surprise start that capped off a really good week for Brandon Woods.

Here's a basic but distressing fact about the good times in our lives: They don't last. We may laugh in the sunshine today, but we do so while we symbolically glance over a shoulder. The Cavs pull off the upset today and then turn around and lose later. We know that sometime – maybe tomorrow – we will cry in the rain as the good times suddenly come crashing down around us.

Awareness of the certainty that good times don't endure often drives many of us to lose our lives and our souls in a lifestyle devoted to the frenetic pursuit of "fun." This is nothing more, though, than a frantic, pitiable, and doomed effort to outrun the bad times lurking around the corner.

The good times will come and go. Only when we quit chasing the good times and instead seek the good life through Jesus Christ do we discover an eternity in which the good times will never end. Only then will we be forever joyous.

*My wife doesn't care what I do when I'm away as long as I don't have a good time.*
*— Hall-of-Fame golfer Lee Trevino*

**Let the good times roll – forever and ever
for the followers of Jesus Christ.**

DAY 57

# RAIN CHECK

### Read Genesis 9:8-17.

*"I establish my covenant with you: Never again will all life be cut off by the waters of a flood; never again will there be a flood to destroy the earth" (v. 11).*

The Cavs were just flat getting worn out by Duke when something wonderful happened: It started raining.

The 1995 Cavaliers were 5-2 with Texas, FSU, Maryland, and Va. Tech dead ahead. A loss at home to Duke, a 22 1/2 point underdog, was unthinkable with the four tough teams still to play.

So everything seemed all right when the Cavs took an early 3-0 lead. But, as defensive tackle Todd White put it, "It seemed everything was going pretty smoothly. Then bam, bam, bam, and it was 21-3." It was indeed.

The Cavs recovered somewhat when quarterback Mike Groh and wide-out Pete Allen teamed up for an 82-yard touchdown bomb. (Groh and Allen would repeat the feat in the Peach Bowl that season, their 82-yard hookup still the longest touchdown pass in UVa bowl history.) Despite that success, Groh was only 3-of-15 passing with two interceptions in the early going.

Then came the rain, and everybody knew the win was in the bag. "We play better in the rain," head coach George Welsh said. They did.

Groh passed for a school-record 346 yards, tailback Tiki Barber rushed for 185 yards, and the 19th-ranked Cavs rallied for

a 44-30 win. "It's a good thing I'm slippery when wet," Barber said after he had accounted for 255 all-purpose yards, the most by a Cavalier in 27 years. "At least what's what [quarterback Mike] Groh told me." Across the way, the Blue Devils were grumbling about the rain. "I thought the ball came back a little wet a few times," said the Duke quarterback.

After their day spent singing in the rain, the Cavs were off and running to a 9-4 season and a Peach-Bowl win over Georgia.

The kids are on go for their picnic. Your golf game is set. You have rib eyes and smoked sausage ready for the grill when the gang comes over tonight. And then it rains.

Sometimes you can slog on through a downpour as the Cavs did against Duke. Often, however, the rain simply washes away your carefully laid plans, and you can't do anything about it.

Rain falls when and where it wants to without checking with you. It answers only to God, the one who controls the heavens from which it comes, the ground on which it falls, and everything in between -- territory that should include you. Though God has absolute dominance over the rain, he will take control of your life only if you let him. In daily seeking his will for your life, you discover that you can live so as to be walking in the sunshine even when it's raining.

*Don't pray when it rains if you don't pray when the sun shines.*
*-- Pitcher and philosopher Leroy "Satchel" Paige*

**Rain falls into every life,**
**but you can live in the glorious light**
**of God's love even during a downpour.**

DAY 58

# FEAR FACTOR

### Read Matthew 14:22-33.

*"[The disciples] cried out in fear. But Jesus immediately
said to them: 'Take courage! It is I. Don't be afraid'" (vv.
26-27).*

**C**oach Terry Holland was notorious for pulling off Halloween
pranks in his gorilla suit.

Holland is the winningest coach in the history of UVa men's
basketball. From 1974-90, he coached the man to 326 wins and a
pair of Final Fours. "I often dressed up in a gorilla suit and trick-
or-treated both the men's and women's teams," he recalled.
Holland couldn't pull his stunt every year since it wouldn't be
effective, but he did pull out the suit on a fairly regular basis.

Heidi Burge was his target in 1989 after coach Debbie Ryan
said she was her team's most timid freshman. Heidi, of course, at
the time teamed with her sister Heather to comprise the tallest
female twins in the world at 6'5". Ryan ensured Heidi had her back
turned when Holland crept up at practice. "All of a sudden, I really
did feel a presence behind me," Burge said. "Like a big grizzly
bear was coming up behind me." Then she saw her teammates'
faces, "and their eyes got really big." Before she could turn her
head, Holland grabbed her. Burge was startled, but nothing like
her teammates, who "scattered, screaming bloody murder."

The team's reaction was nothing like that of Anthony Oliver's.
Holland had an assistant send Oliver (See Devotion No. 46.) into

the locker room one day where the coach lurked in his gorilla outfit with the lights out. When Oliver turned on the lights, Holland jumped out from behind the door.

The prank always frightened Holland's victims and amused him. This time, though, he got more than he bargained for when Oliver passed out and collapsed onto the floor in a heap. That "scared me almost as badly as I had scared him," Holland said.

Some fears are universal; others are particular. Making a speech to a civic group, for instance, may require a heavy dose of antiperspirant. Elevator walls may feel as though they're closing in on you. And don't even get started on being in the dark with spiders and snakes during a thunderstorm.

We all live in fear, which is different from being momentarily startled. God knows about our fears. Dozens of passages in the Bible urge us not to be afraid. God isn't telling us to lose our wariness of oncoming cars or big dogs with nasty dispositions; this is a helpful fear God instilled in us for protection.

What God does wish driven from our lives is a spirit of fear that dominates us, that makes our lives miserable and keeps us from doing what we should, such as sharing our faith. In commanding that we not be afraid, God reminds us that when we trust completely in him, we find peace that calms our fears.

*I was thoroughly shook up for a second.*
*-- Heidi Burge on Terry Holland's Halloween prank*

**You have your own peculiar set of fears,
but they should never paralyze you
because God is greater than anything you fear.**

# CLOTHES HORSE

**Read Genesis 37:1-11.**

*"Israel loved Joseph more than all his children, because he was the son of his old age: and he made him a coat of many colours" (v. 3 KJV).*

**A**ll it took was a bright scarf to determine forever the University of Virginia's school colors.

College football was pretty much a fad among the Ivy League schools until it suddenly spread across the country in the 1880s and 1890s. Virginia's students caught the fever and organized the first official squad in 1888. (See Devotion No. 1.)

Those early UVa teams were coached by students, either the team captain or the manager, a practice that was quite common. The sport drew little interest outside the school in the early days. In fact, it was about seven years after the first official Virginia football team took the field that newspapers did any significant reporting of the games.

A key factor in organizing a school team was the selection of the school colors. The earliest UVa teams wore uniforms of silver gray and cardinal red, their inspiration being the Confederate army's gray uniforms stained with blood. A problem arose, however, when the team played on a muddy field; the colors didn't stand out enough for the fans to discern what was happening.

So before the 1889 season began, the student athletic association held a meeting to select new colors. Allen Potts, one of the school's more outstanding athletes and a member of the first football team, showed up for the meeting wearing a bright scarf of orange and blue that he had bought while on a summer boating expedition at Oxford University. A fellow student grabbed the scarf, waved it around, and asked, "How will this do?"

It did quite well; orange and blue it was.

We know that the colors of the Cavalier uniforms don't determine how well they play. Still, contemporary society proclaims that it's all about the clothes Buy that new suit or dress, those new shoes, and all the sparkling accessories, and you'll be a new person. The changes are only cosmetic, though; under those clothes, you're the same person. Consider Joseph, prancing about in his pretty new clothes; he was still a spoiled little tattletale whom his brothers detested enough to sell into slavery.

Jesus never taught that we should run around half-naked or wear only second-hand clothes from the local mission. He did warn us, though, against making consumer items such as clothes a priority in our lives. A follower of Christ seeks to emulate Jesus not through material, superficial means such as wearing special clothing like a robe and sandals. Rather, the disciple desires to match Jesus' inner beauty and serenity -- whether the clothes the Christian wears are the sables of a king or the rags of a pauper.

*You can't call [golf] a sport. You don't run, jump, you don't shoot, you don't pass. All you have to do is buy some clothes that don't match.*
                                    *-- Former major leaguer Steve Sax*

**Where Jesus is concerned,
clothes don't make the person; faith does.**

# PRACTICE SESSION

**Read 2 Peter 1:3-11.**

*"For if you do these things, you will never fail, and you
will receive a rich welcome into the eternal kingdom of our
Lord and Savior Jesus Christ" (vv. 10b-11).*

George Welsh was so serious about practice that he routinely
tossed players and coaches alike who weren't matching his intensity off the practice field.

Welsh, of course, is the winningest coach in Cavalier football
history, a member of the College Football Hall of Fame and a
coaching legend. A key to his unprecedented success at Virginia
was his approach to practice. "Practice was the most important
thing to George," said longtime assistant coach Danny Wilmer.
"He honestly felt that if you practiced every play like you're in a
game, you would win."

Wilmer said Welsh never hesitated to throw anybody out of
practice who wasn't serious enough for him, including Cavalier
legend Tiki Barber. Once, Wilmer said, the head Cav threw both
the offense and defensive first teams and the entire coaching staff
off the field and made them stand on the sidelines.

Welsh admitted that Wilmer was not exaggerating. "Yeah, I
used to send [players or coaches] over to the sidelines and tell
them, 'When you're ready to practice, you can come back on the
field.'" It usually didn't take long, especially when Welsh added,
"I'll wait for you because I don't have anything else to do tonight."

# CAVALIERS

Welsh's intensity once led to a broken ankle at practice. He was demonstrating a roll out to his quarterback on a wet field, slipped, and got stepped on by his pulling guard. "I didn't demonstrate anymore," he said. Soon after that, when UVa played UNC, Tar Heel head coach Dick Crum and he made history when they met for the post-game handshake: They both were on crutches.

Imagine a football team that never practices. A play cast that doesn't rehearse. A preacher who never reviews or practices his sermon beforehand. When the showdown comes, they would be revealed as inept bumblers who merit our disdain.

We practice something so that we will become good at it, so that it becomes so natural we can pull it off without even having to think about it. Interestingly, if we are to live as Christ wants us to, then we must practice that lifestyle – and showing up at church and sitting stoically on a pew once a week does not constitute practice. To practice successfully, we must participate, we must do repeatedly whatever it is we want to be good at.

We must practice being like Christ by living like Christ every day of our lives. For Christians, practice is a lifestyle that doesn't make perfect -- only Christ is perfect – but it does prepare us for the real thing: the day we meet God face to face and inherit Christ's kingdom.

*You play like you practice and you practice like you play.*
*-- George Welsh*

**Practicing the Christian lifestyle doesn't make us perfect, but it does secure us a permanent place beside the perfect one.**

# VIRGINIA

## DAY 61

## MISTAKE PRONE

### Read Mark 14:66-72.

*"Then Peter remembered the word Jesus had spoken to
him: 'Before the rooster crows twice you will disown me
three times.' And he broke down and wept" (v. 72).*

**C**avalier quarterback Matt Blundin made mistakes during the
1991 season, as any player does. His errors, however, did not include throwing interceptions. He didn't have a single one all year
long, setting an NCAA record in the process.

Blundin is the only UVa athlete in history to play in a football
bowl game (1991) and in the NCAA Tournament's Elite Eight
(1989). His only start as a junior in 1990 was against Virginia Tech.
"It was a very low point for me," Blundin said about the game. He
passed for a career-high 305 yards but threw three interceptions
in the last half as the Hokies won easily.

Blundin's senior year was a different matter entirely, however,
especially when it came to interceptions. Those interceptions he
threw against Tech were the last ones he ever tossed in a collegiate regular season game. A bacterial infection in his throwing
arm sidelined him for a pair of games early in the season, but
when he came back, the result was a run to the Gator Bowl and
the NCAA record book.

Blundin's college career came full circle when he faced Virginia
Tech in 1991 and threw for 222 yards and three touchdowns and
didn't throw an interception. He thus finished the season with

224 passes without a pick, a major college record.

Like Blundin, UVa made few mistakes that day. In routing the Hokies 38-0, the Cavs handed Tech its worst loss in almost a decade. It was Virginia's greatest margin of victory since a 42-0 beatdown of Tech in 1952.

It's distressing but it's true: Like Cavalier football players and Simon Peter, we all make mistakes. Only one perfect man ever walked on this earth, and no one of us is he. Some mistakes are just dumb. Like locking yourself out of your car or falling into a swimming pool with your clothes on.

Other mistakes are more significant. Like heading down a path to addiction. Committing a crime. Walking out on a spouse and the children.

All these mistakes, however, from the momentarily annoying to the life-altering tragic, share one aspect: They can all be forgiven in Christ. Other folks may not forgive us; we may not even forgive ourselves. But God will forgive us when we call upon him in Jesus' name.

Thus, the twofold fatal mistake we can make is ignoring the fact that we will die one day and subsequently ignoring the fact that Jesus is the only way to shun Hell and enter Heaven. We absolutely must get this one right.

*In the beginning of the game, the record wasn't that meaningful. But, as the game went along, it felt good to have it under my belt.*
*-- Matt Blundin on setting the record for not throwing interceptions*

**Only one mistake we make sends us to Hell**
**when we die: ignoring Jesus while we live.**

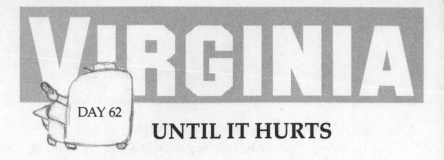

# UNTIL IT HURTS

**Read 1 Peter 4:12-19.**

*"Rejoice that you participate in the sufferings of Christ, so that you may be overjoyed when his glory is revealed"*
*(v. 13).*

Former Cav basketball coach Jeff Jones conducted a post-game interview in great pain in 1994, and his self-inflicted injury became a source of superstition for his doctor.

Jones was a four-year starter at point guard for the Cavs from 1978-82. He set school records for career assists (598) and assists in a season, both marks later broken by John Crotty. In 1990, he became the Cavs' eighth head coach and led the team for eight seasons that included five trips to the NCAA, an ACC regular-season championship, and four 20-win campaigns.

In the '94 season finale, the Cavs lost to Maryland 70-68. Jones vented his frustration in the dressing room by slamming a fist into a blackboard against a cinder block wall. "I heard a crack," he said -- and it wasn't the blackboard. Refusing to let his players know he had hurt himself, Jones whispered to trainer Ethan Saliba, "I need ice and pain pills . . . fast." By the time Jones showed up for his post-game interview, reporters could see that his hand was swelling and that he was gamely trying to mask his pain.

A visit to legendary team doctor Frank McCue verified that his hand was broken. "He puts a cast on it, said it was a clean break and said it should heal in about four weeks," Jones said.

The hand healed quickly, but each week when Jones visited McCue, the doctor said, "Leave it on." Jones pretty much knew why he kept the cast: The break coincided with a hot postseason streak. The Cavs toppled Maryland and 5th-ranked Duke in the ACC Tournament to earn a berth in the NCAA tourney. They then upset New Mexico 57-54 in the first round before falling to 9th-ranked Arizona. "It's amazing to me how quickly after we lost to Arizona that I was healed up," Jones said with a smile.

We don't usually include actual physical pain and suffering as part of the price we are willing to pay to succeed. We'll work overtime, we may neglect our family, we may even work ourselves into exhaustion, but actual pain, suffering, and agony? They are definitely not part of our job description. What would we give up to avoid pain and suffering whether on the job or in our daily lives? Everything?

Merely by choosing to, Jesus could have easily evaded the horrific pain and suffering he underwent. Instead, he opted for his love for you over his own well-being, and agony was part of his decision for love.

Now we all face the question: How far do we go with Jesus? Do we bail out on him when it gets inconvenient? Or do we walk with him all the way even when it hurts – just as Jesus did for us?

*Sometimes you have to play with a little pain.*
*-- Clemson running back C.J. Spiller*

**We must decide whether we'll walk all the way**
**with Jesus, even when it hurts, or whether**
**we'll bail out when faith gets inconvenient.**

DAY 63

# YOUNG BLOOD

### Read Jeremiah 1:4-10.

*"The Lord said to me, 'Do not say, 'I am only a child' . . .
for I am with you and will rescue you" (vv. 7a, 8).*

In 1958, a young coach just starting out got his first job as an assistant at the University of Virginia. That youngster went on to become a coaching legend. He was Don Shula.

Shula was 28 when the school announced on Feb. 18, 1958, that he had joined the staff of head coach Dick Voris as the secondary coach. He landed the job through a coaching friend of Voris', accepting an offer over the phone. That summer, he married the woman who would be his wife until her death in 1991. They packed everything they owned into a 15957 Mercury, went on a honeymoon, and moved into an apartment near Memorial Gym.

As he did everywhere he went in his Hall-of-Fame coaching career, Shula made an immediate impression -- certainly on UVa great Sonny Randle. "Now, Sonny, he was my guy," Shula once said. Randle wasn't so sure. Shula wanted Randle in his secondary, but, as Randle put it, "I wouldn't hit anybody."

At the Monday practice following the season-opening loss to Clemson, a bruised and battered Randle stayed on the sideline when coaches called for the first team. Shula would have none of it. "What's wrong with you?" he bellowed right in front of everybody. Randle rolled off a litany of ailments: ankle, knee, thigh, ankle bruise.

# CAVALIERS

Then came Shula's reply. "I'm going to tell you something, son. Anybody can play when there's nothing wrong with them, but you separate the good ones from the bad ones when you can play hurt." Randle said, he got "a whole lot better in a hurry."

Randle, who went on to an 11-year NFL career and coached for two seasons in Charlottesville, later said that the intense young coach "was the best thing to happen to me." He told folks, "Boy, he'll be a short-timer here." Shula moved on after the '58 season.

While the media seem inordinately obsessed with youth, most aspects of our society value experience and some hard-won battle scars. Life usually requires us to spend time on the bench as a reserve, waiting for our chance to play with the big boys and girls. You probably rode some pine in high school. You started college as a lowly freshman. You began work at an entry-level position. Even legendary football coaches learn their trade as assistants.

Paying your dues is traditional, but that should never stop you from doing something bold right away. Nowhere is this truer than in your faith life.

You may well assert that you are too young and too inexperienced to really do anything for God. Those are just excuses, however, and God won't pay a lick of attention to them when he issues a call.

After all, being young just gives you more time to serve God.

*It was my first coaching job. How could I forget?*
*-- Don Shula on his year at UVa*

**Youth is no excuse for not serving God;
it just gives you more time.**

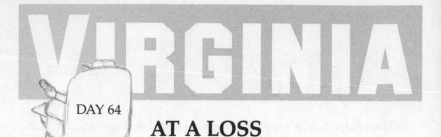
DAY 64

# AT A LOSS

### Read Philippians 3:1-9.

*"I consider everything a loss compared to the surpassing greatness of knowing Christ Jesus my Lord, for whose sake I have lost all things" (v. 8).*

The Cavaliers surrendered the most points in George Welsh's nineteen seasons at the UVa helm and lost by 48 points, but the most painful loss that weekend didn't take place on the field.

Craig Fielder was a defensive back who was redshirted in the fall of 1984. During his second semester, he developed a persistent cough and eventually went to a doctor. It wasn't pneumonia as everyone had thought; Fielder had a virulent form of cancer.

After chemotherapy, he rejoined the team for spring practice in 1986; he lettered that season, playing in all 11 games and being on the field for 153 plays. But the cancer returned; Fielder's roommate, Chris Kite, was riding with him to Scott Stadium when Fielder told his friend he had only eight to twelve weeks to live.

A doctor gave Fielder permission to travel with the team to the South Carolina game of Oct. 17, 1987. "We weren't so sure it was a good idea to go, but he wanted to and the team said that was fine," recalled Fielder's mother. "When he showed up for the plane, I was struck by how weak he was," Welsh said.

Strength and conditioning coach John Gamble asked if he could room with Fielder on the trip. Shortly after they arrived in the room, Fielder started having trouble breathing. Gamble sent

someone for the team physician, and he held Fielder as he died. "It was just hard. I cried all night," Gamble said.

After dinner, Welsh called the players together and told them that Fielder had died. "I thought it was important that we tell them that night and not wait till the morning," the head man said. But, he added, "There was no way to play football that day." Not when losing a game wasn't as important as the loss the team had already suffered.

Maybe, as it was with the 1987 UVa football team, it was when a family member died. Perhaps it wasn't so staggeringly tragic: your puppy died, your best friend moved away, or an older sibling left home. Sometime in your youth or early adult life, though, you learned that loss is a part of life.

Loss inevitably diminishes your life, but loss and the grief that accompanies it are part of the price of loving. When you first encountered loss, you learned that you were virtually helpless to prevent it or escape it.

There is life after loss, though, because you have a sure place to turn. Jesus can share your pain and ease your suffering; but he doesn't stop there. Through the loss of his own life, he has transformed death -- the ultimate loss -- into the ultimate gain of eternal life. In Jesus lies the promise that one day loss itself will die.

*I don't think we were going to win anyway.*
*-- George Welsh on how the loss affected UVa's play against USC*

**Jesus not only eases the pain of our losses**
**but transforms the loss caused by death**
**into the gain of eternal life.**

DAY 65

# FOOD FOR THOUGHT

**Read Genesis 9:1-7.**

*"Everything that lives and moves will be food for you. Just as I gave you the green plants, I now give you everything"* *(v. 3).*

Former UVa player and head football coach Al Groh once got thrown out of a Cavalier lacrosse match, but he got a free lunch out of the deal.

Groh coached the Cavs from 2000-2009 and was twice the ACC Coach of the Year. He was a defensive end on the UVa football team from 1963-65 and also lettered in lacrosse.

As Groh recalled it, "I played on one of the historically bad Virginia lacrosse teams and one of the reasons it was bad was because I was playing on it." Groh said his stickwork was so un-sophisticated that he could have played with an oar and done as well. As the team's designated crease defenseman, Groh's job was to move offensive players out of the crease so the goalie wasn't shielded. "I was kind of a designated goon," Groh said.

In a contest against Yale, Groh took offense at a rather nasty stick to the face, a foul that wasn't called. He knocked the offending Yale player to his back, straddled him, and started pounding on him. The officials were Groh's history teacher and Bob Sandell, the lacrosse head coach at UVa from 1955-58 and for years a lacrosse and basketball official and an ACC football official. They threw Groh out of the game for fighting.

The next day Groh and some teammates visited the local Dairy Queen, which Sandell owned. His eye swollen shut from the blow from the stick, Groh told him, "Mr. Sandell, I just wanted you to know I didn't start the fight yesterday." Sandell was horror-struck and felt so bad that he gave Groh lunch on the house. The two remained friends until Sandell's death in January 2011.

Belly up to the buffet, boys and girls, for barbecue, sirloin steak, grilled chicken, and fried catfish with hush puppies and cheese grits. Rachael Ray's a household name; hamburger joints, pizza parlors, and taco stands lurk on every corner; and we have television channels devoted exclusively to food. We love our chow.

Food is one of God's really good ideas, but consider the complex divine plan that begins with a seed and ends with French fries. The creator of all life devised a system in which living things are sustained and nourished physically through the sacrifice of other living things in a way similar to what Christ underwent to save us spiritually. Whether it's fast food or home-cooked, everything we eat is a gift from God secured through a divine plan in which some plants and animals have given up their lives.

Pausing to give thanks before we dive in seems the least we can do.

*What do you want? A hamburger, a vanilla milk shake. Whatever you want, you can have.*

-- *A guilt-ridden Bob Sandell to Al Groh*

**God created a system that nourishes us
through the sacrifice of other living things;
that's worth a thank-you.**

# ANIMAL MAGNETISM

**Read Psalm 139:1-18.**

*"For you created my inmost being; you knit me together in my mother's womb. I praise you because I am fearfully and wonderfully made" (vv. 13-14).*

Today, the mounted Cavalier leads the Virginia football team onto the field at home games, and the costumed Cavalier with its large character head entertains at various functions and serves as the official school mascot. Once upon a time, though, two mongrel dogs achieved fame as Virginia's first mascots.

The first-ever UVa mascot was a black-and-white mutt named Beta. In the 1920s and '30s, Beta was so beloved he was virtually considered a member of the student body. History recalls that he attended a course on Plato so frequently that the professor added his name to the roll and called it as with other students. Beta always answered with a robust bark. He became quite famous, earning a mention on a nationwide radio broadcast and appearing in *Look* magazine. On April 6, 1939, Beta was struck by a car and had to be put to sleep.

Another mutt continued the tradition of dog mascots in the 1940s. He was cross-eyed but had such a sleek coat of fur that he was named Seal. Like his predecessor, Seal was welcome in UVa lecture halls and nearly everywhere around town.

Seal achieved fame to match that of Beta during halftime of the 1949 Penn game in Philadelphia. Wearing a blue blanket em-

CAVALIERS

bossed with an orange "V," Seal walked over to where the Penn cheerleaders had placed their megaphones. According to the *Cavalier Daily*, he inspected the "cheerleading appurtenances. Eighty thousand people watched with bated breath. Coolly, insolently, Seal lifted a leg -- the rest is history." UVa won 26-14, and Seal became known as Caninus Megaphonus Pennsylvanus.

Animals such as the Cavalier's horse and lovable characters such as Beta and Seal elicit both our awe and our respect. Nothing enlivens a trip more than glimpsing turkeys, bears, or deer in the wild. Admit it: You go along with the kids' trip to the zoo because you think it's a cool place too. All that variety of life is mind-boggling. Who could conceive of a walrus, a moose, or a prairie dog? Who could possibly have that rich an imagination?

But the next time you're in a crowd, look around at the parade of faces. Who could come up with the idea for all those different people? For that matter, who could conceive of you? You are unique, a masterpiece who will never be duplicated.

The master creator, God Almighty, is behind it all. He thought of you and brought you into being. If you had a manufacturer's label, it might say, "Lovingly, fearfully, and wonderfully handmade in Heaven by #1 -- God."

*Local restaurants with signs reading, "No Dogs Allowed," would write below, in parentheses, "except Seal."*

*-- VirginiaSports.com*

**You may consider some painting
or a magnificent animal a work of art,
but the real masterpiece is you.**

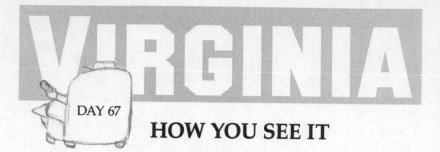

# HOW YOU SEE IT

**Read John 20:11-18.**

*"Mary stood outside the tomb crying" (v. 11).*

She's absolutely been amazing in her perspective. She's been a great, great inspiration to me, and, I think, to her family and to her teammates."

So spoke Mark Bernardino, longtime head coach of Virginia's powerhouse men's and women's swimming programs. The athlete who impressed him with her perspective on life was swimmer Claire Crippen. Crippen is one of the school's greatest swimmers ever. She entered her senior season of competition in 2010-11 as a team captain, a three-time honorable mention All-America, a two-time ACC champion in the 400-yard individual medley, and the school record-holder in the event.

Crippen's perspective revealed itself in the relaxed demeanor she displayed even in the block immediately before a race. "She never stops smiling, she never stops laughing," Bernardino said of her. It's not that Crippen wasn't serious about swimming; her success demonstrates her total dedication to the sport. Rather, as Bernardino said, "You'll never find a more positive, happy, outgoing person. You can't take the joy out of her heart."

Many people -- especially Christians -- walk around with a smile and a joyous outlook. So what made Claire Crippen's positive perspective so impressive to Bernardino and her teammates? It's that she maintained it in the wake of deep personal tragedy.

# CAVALIERS

Her older brother, Fran, is a UVa swimming legend. He was the ACC swimmer of the year in 2003 and 2004, an eight-time ACC champion, and 11-time All-America. He was so successful that Claire was wary of following him to Charlottesville because she didn't want to be compared to him.

They were close. She thinks of him every time she steps on the block for a race. And on Oct. 23, 2010, at age 26, Fran died while competing in an open-water race near Dubai.

Your perspective goes a long way toward determining whether you slink through life amid despair, anger, and hopelessness or stride boldly through life with joy and hope as Claire Crippen does. Mary is a good example also. On that first Easter morning, she stood by Jesus' tomb crying, her heart broken, because she still viewed everything through the perspective of Jesus' death. But how her attitude, her heart, and her life changed when she saw the morning through the perspective of Jesus' resurrection.

So it is with life and death for all of us. You can't avoid death, but you can determine how you perceive it. Is it fearful, dark, fraught with peril and uncertainty? Or is it a simple little passageway to glory, the light, and loved ones, an elevator ride to paradise?

It's a matter of perspective that depends totally on whether or not you're standing by Jesus' side when it arrives.

*She just finds the good in everything that you can find good in. She searches for good.*
*— Mark Bernardino on Claire Crippen's perspective on life*

**Whether death is your worst enemy or a solicitous chauffeur is a matter of perspective.**

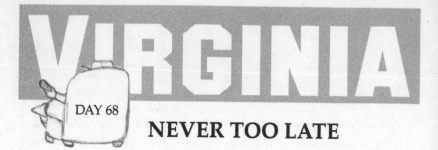

## DAY 68

# NEVER TOO LATE

**Read Genesis 21:1-7.**

*"And [Sarah] added, 'Who would have said to Abraham that Sarah would nurse children? Yet I have borne him a son in his old age'" (v. 7).*

The Cavs proved against Clemson that it's never too late to pull out a win. All you need is one second.

On Sept. 22, 2001, the 1-1 Cavs took on 19th-ranked Clemson in Death Valley. The Tigers jumped out to a 10-0 lead before the Cavs rallied to lead 20-10 in the third quarter. But the momentum shifted again as Clemson put together a rally to take a 24-20 lead. UVa got a huge play when cornerback Muffin Curry blitzed and sacked the Clemson quarterback, forcing a fumble. Defensive tackle Larry Simmons gathered up the ball and rumbled 26 yards to the Tiger 34 with 4:52 to play.

A holding penalty backed UVa up and forced a punt with the clock down to 3:28. Punter Mike Abrams, the lone player from South Carolina on UVa's roster, lofted a cloud bumper that tail-back Marquis Weeks downed at the Clemson 4.

The Tigers tried three running plays, but the UVa defense refused to budge, forcing a fourth-down punt with 1:44 on the clock. The Cavs got a big break on the kick, which was short and went out of bounds at the Clemson 44. Quarterback Bryson Spinner picked up 7 yards on a first-down run. Junior wide receiver Billy McMullen, who from 1999-2002 set the school career records for both receptions and receiving yards, hauled in a pair of passes down to the Clemson 4. McMullen's 83 catches in 2001 still stand as the school record for a season. The latter pass was thrown by back Tyree Foreman, who took the Cavs to the 1 with a pair of runs. With six seconds left, Spinner lifted a lob in the general direction of the 6-foot-4 McMullen, who hauled it in for a touchdown and the 26-24 win.

And not a bit too soon; the clock had one tick left.

Getting that college degree. Getting married. Starting a new career. Though we may make all kinds of excuses, it's often never too late for life-changing decisions and milestones.

This is especially true in our faith life, which is based on God's promises. Abraham was 100 and Sarah was 90 when their first child was born. They were old folks even by the Bible's standards at the dawn of history. But God had promised them a child and just as God always does, he kept his promise no matter how unlikely it seemed.

God has made us all a promise of new life and hope through Jesus Christ. At any time in our lives – today even -- we can regret the things we have done wrong and the way we have lived, ask God in Jesus' name to forgive us for them, and discover a new way of living – forever.

It's never too late to change. God promised.

*It's never too late to achieve success in sports.*
       *-- Brooke de Lench, writer and lecturer on children and sports*

**It's never too late to change a life
by turning it over to Jesus.**

# VIRGINIA

## FAMILY TIES

**Read Mark 3:31-35.**

*"[Jesus] said, 'Here are my mother and my brothers!
Whoever does God's will is my brother and sister and
mother'" (vv. 34-35).*

If Branden Albert ever wants to give a testimony about the positive influences in his life, he might well start with a parole officer.

At 6-7 and 300 lbs., Albert started every game during his career at Virginia (2005-07), mostly as a guard. He was only the second UVa freshman since 1972 to start on the offensive line, was All-ACC in 2006, and was the fifteenth player taken in the 2008 NFL draft. He was an immediate starter in the pros as a rookie.

Albert was never a disciplinary problem requiring a personal parole officer, but his life would certainly have been different were it not for his older brother. He was pretty much going nowhere in high school in Rochester, N.Y. He failed the ninth grade because "I was a very lazy kid when it came to schoolwork," he said. Albert was in the process of failing the ninth grade again and on a sure path to dropping out when his mother decided he needed some tough love. She sent him to live with his brother, Ashley Sims, who was a Baltimore parole and probation officer and a former football player for the University of Maryland.

"My brother was very tough on me," Albert recalled. Sims laid down the rules: "Do well in school, clean up behind yourself, respect me and my wife," and play football. "He kind of frowned

# CAVALIERS

when I told him the [football] part," Sims said. Albert didn't exactly have what Sims called the "football fever" until he took his younger brother to Maryland's football camp before Albert's junior year. "It kind up woke him up then and there," Sims said. "After that, he became a football jock."

And an all-star and professional football player thanks largely to guidance from his brother the parole officer.

Some wit said families are like fudge, mostly sweet with a few nuts. You can probably call the names of your sweetest relatives, whom you cherish, and of the nutty ones too, whom you mostly try to avoid at a family reunion.

Like it or not, you have a family, and that's God's doing. God cherishes the family so much that he chose to live in one as a son, a brother, and a cousin.

One of Jesus' more startling actions was to redefine the family. No longer is it a single household of blood relatives or even a clan or a tribe. Jesus' family is the result not of an accident of birth but rather a conscious choice. All those who do God's will are members of Jesus' family.

What a startling and downright wonderful thought! You have family members out there you don't even know who stand ready to love you just because you're part of God's family.

*The first couple of months, he'd get home from work and sit me down at the table, like a little kid, till I finished my homework.*
*-- Branden Albert on his brother's emphasis on schoolwork*

**For followers of Jesus, family comes not from a shared ancestry but from a shared faith.**

DAY 70

# DRY RUN

### Read John 4:1-15.

*"Everyone who drinks this water will be thirsty again,
but whoever drinks the water I give him will never thirst.
Indeed, the water I give him will become in him a spring
of water welling up to eternal life" (vv. 13-14).*

The drought was of Biblical proportions. Virginia had not beaten Virginia Tech in ten tries.

The Wahoos owned their counterparts from Blacksburg in the early years of the series, winning the first eight encounters by a combined 170-5 score. The dominance continued on into 1927 with a 7-0 win that gave Virginia an 11-3 edge against their bitter rivals. No one would have dreamed that more than a decade would pass before the Wahoos would beat Tech again. Three ties was all UVa could muster during that stretch, two of them by an uninspiring 0-0 count.

After the 1935 scoreless tie, the UVa campus paper published a joke in which one fan asked another if he were attending the Virginia game today. The other Wahoo, grammatically inspired, replied, "Why, you don't attend games, you attend funerals." The first fan countered, "Well, they're all the same here at Virginia."

The situation was so bad that the same student newspaper moaned, "Never, since its dedication in 1926, have the Cavaliers succeeded in defeating the Gobblers on their home field." As the 1938 season unrolled, it didn't appear this would be the year the

# CAVALIERS

drought would end. When the team arrived in Blacksburg for the game, they were greeted by an effigy of a dead Cavalier hanging in front of the student activity building.

It turned out, though, that the Cavs had been given up for dead a little prematurely. Junior back Jimmy Gillette scored two touchdowns to lead Virginia to a 14-6 win, which, that same pessimistic student paper said, "shattered an 11-year session of Polytechnic domination." The drought was over.

You can walk across that river you boated on in the spring. The city's put all neighborhoods on water restriction. That beautiful lawn you fertilized and seeded will turn a sickly, pale green and may lapse all the way to brown. Somebody wrote "Wash Me" on the rear window of your truck.

The sun bakes everything, including the concrete. The earth itself seems exhausted, just barely hanging on. It's a drought.

It's the way a soul that shuts God out looks.

God instilled thirst in us to warn us of our body's need for physical water. He also gave us a spiritual thirst that can be quenched only by his presence in our lives. Without God, we are like tumbleweeds, dried out and windblown, offering the illusion of life where there is only death.

Living water – water of life – is readily available in Jesus. We may drink our fill, and thus we slake our thirst and end our soul's drought – forever.

*Drink before you are thirsty. Rest before you are tired.*
*-- Paul de Vivie, father of French cycle touring*

**Our soul thirsts for God's refreshing presence.**

# WATER POWER

**Read Acts 10:34-48.**

*"Can anyone keep these people from being baptized with water? They have received the Holy Spirit just as we have" (v. 47).*

The two head coaches moved into what is probably the finest college basketball arena in America, one with a price tag of some $150 million -- and they wanted to talk about their showers.

Virginia's basketball showpiece, John Paul Jones Arena, opened for basketball business with the start of the 2006-07 season. Few expenses were spared and no corners were cut. "Just looking around here right now, it gives me chills," said senior guard J.R. Reynolds about his new playhouse.

Reynolds' backcourt partner, Sean Singletary, liked the new place all right, but said he'd miss old University Hall. "It was a great home for basketball," he said, though Singletary admitted he wouldn't miss the constant rescheduling of practices required because the team shared the lone floor with the women. Now, in the arena, each team has a practice gym. "I've never seen anything like it," Reynolds said. "Some NBA arenas don't even have that."

The offices for head coaches Dave Leitao and Debbie Ryan were as palatial as the rest of the facility. "It's quiet, it's private, it's got great acoustics," Leitao said about his man-cave. "It's like a laboratory or a professor with his classroom." But what floored Leitao the most was one amenity he never imagined he would

have: his own shower in the office. "I'm almost humbled by it," he said. "How many people have a shower in their office?"

Ryan does. She who once had an office beneath the steps at University Hall felt she was moving into a mansion. "My office is so big," she said, "that we're trying to figure out a way to get the echo out of it." Like Leitao, the shower impressed her, though she did notice that her shower head "was about 20 feet off the ground." She figured the designers thought all 7'4" of Cavalier basketball great Ralph Sampson would be showering in there.

It's not just showers and tubs. If there's any water around we'll probably be in it, on it, or near it. Children's wading pools and swimming pools in the backyard. Fishing, boating, skiing, and swimming at a lake. Sun, sand, and surf at the beach. If there's not any water at hand, we'll build a dam and create our own.

We love the wet stuff for its recreational uses, but water first and foremost is about its absolute necessity to support and maintain life. From its earliest days, the Christian church appropriated water as an image of life through the ritual of baptism. Since the time of the arrival of the Holy Spirit at Pentecost, baptism with water has been the symbol of entry into the Christian community. It is water that marks a person as belonging to Jesus. It is through water that a person proclaims that Jesus is his Lord.

There's something in the water, all right. There is life.

*He's big time with that shower.*
*— Boston College coach Al Skinner on Dave Leitao's favorite amenity*

**There is life in the water:**
**physical life and spiritual life.**

# VIRGINIA

## DAY 72

# TEARS IN HEAVEN

**Read Revelation 21:1-8.**

*"[God] will wipe every tear from their eyes. There will be no more death or mourning or crying or pain" (v. 4).*

There are tears in football. Just ask quarterback David Rivers.

After the 1999 Georgia Tech game, when Rivers finally reached the locker room "after accepting congratulations from thousands of his newest best friends," he did something he had never done before on the field: He lost control of his emotions, broke down, and cried. Head coach George Welsh knew about the tears, and he was quite happy about them because he knew why Rivers was so emotional.

They weren't tears of despair but rather tears that helped release Rivers from three and one-half seasons of obscurity and frustration. In 1996 as a freshman, Rivers was redshirted. He then spent two seasons as the no. 3 quarterback behind Aaron Brooks and Dan Ellis. In 1999, he moved up to no. 2 behind Ellis but threw only two passes in the first seven and one-half games. When Ellis suffered a concussion against FSU, Rivers was tabbed for his first career start, against Georgia Tech.

In the early going, if any tears were shed, they were indeed signs of despair as the seventh-ranked Yellow Jackets jumped out to a 17-0 lead on their way to an apparent easy victory. But as Welsh put it, "How do you explain athletes when they're 21 years old?" Rivers finished his afternoon by hitting on 10 of 18 passes

# CAVALIERS

for 228 yards and three touchdowns. He completed passes to ten different receivers and led the Cavaliers to a thrilling 45-38 win.

"He threw to the right people when they blitzed and he put the ball on the money," Welsh said of Rivers' play. "After the first quarter, he settled in and threw some bullets." Later that night, ESPN's John Mackovic pulled out a Cavalier helmet and named Rivers his player of the day

When he met the media that night, Rivers explained, "It's been a long four years. It wasn't hard to be overcome by emotion."

When your parents died. When a friend told you she was divorcing. When you broke your collarbone. When you watch a sad movie. You cry. Crying is as much a part of life as are breathing and potholes on the highway. Usually our tears are brought on by pain, sorrow, or disappointment.

But what about when your child was born? When UVa rallies to win? When you discovered Jesus Christ? Those times elicit tears too; we cry at the times of our greatest, most overwhelming joy.

Thus, while there will be tears in Heaven, they will only be tears of sheer, unmitigated, undiluted joy. The greatest joy possible, a joy beyond our imagining, must occur when we finally see Christ. If we shed tears when Virginia wins a game, can we really believe that we will stand dry-eyed and calm in the presence of Jesus?

What we will not shed in Heaven are tears of sorrow and pain.

*He broke down and he deserved his moment of happiness, certainly.*
*-- George Welsh on David Rivers' tears after the Georgia Tech game*

**Tears in Heaven will be like everything else there:
a part of the joy we will experience.**

### DAY 73

# WITNESS PROTECTION

**Read Hebrews 11:39-12:2.**

*"Therefore, since we are surrounded by such a great cloud of witnesses, . . . let us run with perseverance the race marked out for us" (v. 12:1).*

UVa's director of promotions decided to do something about the small crowds attending the women's basketball games. What resulted has only half-seriously been estimated to cost the university more than $10 million.

Women's basketball at UVa was counted among the big-time programs by the 1985-86 season. The team won 20 straight games to start the season and moved to a No. 3 ranking. Still, attendance at the women's games hovered only around 1,000. Director of Promotions Kim Record decided to give the sport a boost by breaking the ACC single-game attendance record. She decided to have a night with free admission, hot dogs, and soft drinks for everyone who showed up.

She chose the Feb. 5 contest against 15th-ranked North Carolina, a big game in itself, and landed a whole bunch of free publicity by arranging a halftime game between members of the media. The buzz spread about what came to be called Hot Dog Night. Eight hours before tipoff, fans were in line. The announced attendance was 11,174, but Record said she thought the crowd was at least 13,000. University Hall could usually squeeze in about 10,000.

Unfortunately, the fire marshal showed up and turned in a re-

# CAVALIERS

port that reduced the gym's permanent seating capacity to 8,392. Years later, men's coach Terry Holland called the night "a huge success in that we set a women's record at that time for attendance." But, he added, "We gave away free hot dogs and free admission to that game to lose 1,800 seats" per night. Over the years, that easily amounted to more than $10 million in lost revenue.

Like the UVa women's basketball team in its early days, you, too, probably don't have a huge crowd of folks daily applauding your efforts. You certainly don't have TV cameras broadcasting your every move to an enthralled audience. Sometimes you may even feel alone. A child's illness, the slow death of a loved one, financial troubles, worries about your health – you feel isolated.

But a person of faith is never alone, and not just because you're aware of God's presence. You are always surrounded by a crowd of God's most faithful witnesses, those in the present and those from the past. Their faithfulness both encourages and inspires. They, too, have faced the difficult circumstances with which you contend, and they remained faithful and true to God.

With their examples before you, you can endure your trials, looking in hope and faithfulness beyond your immediate troubles to God's glorious future. Your final victory in Christ will be even sweeter because of your struggles.

*People were just everywhere. They were hanging off the rafters. It was crazy -- in the bathrooms, in the hallways. Just nuts.*
*– Coach Debbie Ryan on Hot Dog Night*

**The person of faith is surrounded by a crowd of witnesses whose faithfulness in difficult times inspires us to remain true to God no matter what.**

# VIRGINIA

## STRANGE BUT TRUE

**Read Isaiah 9:2-7.**

*"The zeal of the Lord Almighty will accomplish this" (v. 7).*

Strange but true: Frustrated by constant losses to Virginia, a VPI head coach once held a scrimmage to see who really wanted to play -- right before the game.

With head coach Art Guepe on hand from 1946-52, the Cavaliers owned the Hokies from Blacksburg. The only time VPI came close to beating a Guepe-coached UVa team was a 21-21 tie in 1946. Over the next six seasons, Virginia outscored the Hokies 219-13. The score was 41-7 in '47, leaving the stunned VPI head coach to say, "I didn't think it would be like this." The count was 28-0 in 1948 as end Bob "Rock" Weir caught a 57-yard touchdown pass and junior fullback John Papit had a 65-yard run.

The outlook for the Hokies against the Cavaliers didn't look any better in 1949. UVa was again led by Papit, who would earn All-America honors. He rushed for 1,214 yards in '49, a school record that stood until Barry Word broke it with 1,224 yards in 1985. He is still Virginia's fourth all-time leading rusher, and his 224 yards against Washington & Lee in 1948 is still the school record.

Guepe had so much talent on hand that he went to a two-platoon system in '49. Both Cavalier fans and players expected once again to drub VPI. "They were pitiful," Weir recalled. Even Guepe admitted, "We didn't have much trouble with the Gobblers."

# CAVALIERS

In what was apparently a desperate attempt to change VPI's fortunes, the head coach adopted the strange strategy of holding a scrimmage right before kickoff "to see who really wanted to play." It didn't work; Virginia won easily 26-0.

The strange scrimmage left the UVa student paper wondering if the Gobblers "hadn't used up all their energy because their attack went for nil against a solid Cavalier forward wall."

Life is just strange, isn't it? How else to explain the college bowl situation, Dr. Phil, tattoos, curling, tofu, and teenagers? Isn't it strange that today we have more ways to stay in touch with each other yet are losing the intimacy of personal contact?

And how strange is God's plan to save us? Think a minute about what God did. He could have come roaring down, destroying and blasting everyone whose sinfulness offended him, which, of course, is pretty much all of us. Then he could have brushed off his hands, nodded the divine head, and left a scorched planet in his wake. All in a day's work.

Instead, God came up with a totally novel plan: He would save the world by becoming a human being, letting himself be humiliated, tortured, and killed, and thus establishing a kingdom of justice and righteousness that will last forever.

It's a strange way to save the world – but it's true.

*It may sound strange, but many champions are made champions by setbacks.*

*-- Olympic champion Bob Richards*

**It's strange but true: God allowed himself
to be killed on a cross to save the world.**

# VIRGINIA

# THE FAME GAME

## Read 1 Kings 10:1-10, 18-29.

*"King Solomon was greater in riches and wisdom than all the other kings of the earth. The whole world sought audience with Solomon" (vv. 23-24).*

They were so famous that one of them said, "For years, I was pointed out." They were the Cavalier team that beat Yale.

Virginia football was thriving as never before in 1915. Behind legendary halfback Eugene "Buck" Mayer, the first player from a Southern school to be named first-team All-America, the Cavs compiled a 23-3-0 record from 1913-15.

Many historians insist that the 1915 football team with its 8-1 record was the best in Virginia history largely because of what it did on Oct. 3. Until that day, no team from the South had ever beaten a traditional Eastern power, and certainly not Yale. In 40 years of football, nearly 400 games, Yale had lost only 26 times and only nine games outside of Princeton, Penn, and Harvard.

Then the Cavaliers swaggered into town and thoroughly dominated the Elis 10-0. The game was scoreless in the fourth quarter when T.G. Coleman recovered a Yale fumble for a touchdown. Mayer kicked the extra point. After another fumble recovery, Allen Thurman hit a 40-yard drop-kick field goal to end any Yale hopes of a comeback. Yale had just three first downs the whole game and penetrated the UVa 30 only once.

Cavalier lineman Claude Moore said beating Yale was his all-time favorite memory. Instant celebrities, the players were feted in New York City with box seats at a show. Moore said that for years afterward, UVa fans would point at him and say, "He played on the team that beat Yale."

Have you ever wanted to be famous? Hanging out with other rich and famous people, having folks with microphones listen to what you say, throwing money around like toilet paper, meeting adoring and clamoring fans, signing autographs, and posing for the paparazzi before you climb into your imported sports car?

Many of us yearn to be famous, well-known in the places and by the people that we believe matter. That's all fame amounts to: strangers knowing your name and your face.

The truth is that you are already famous where it really does matter, which excludes TV's talking heads, screaming teenagers, rapt moviegoers, or D.C. power brokers. You are famous because Almighty God knows your name, your face, and everything else there is to know about you.

If a persistent photographer snapped you pondering this fame – the only kind that has eternal significance – would the picture show the world unbridled joy or the shell-shocked expression of a mug shot?

*The fans can make you famous. The press can make you a superstar.*
*But only the love can make you a player.*
*-- Soccer player Kevin Hartwyk*

**You're already famous because**
**God knows your name and your face,**
**which may be either reassuring or terrifying.**

## DAY 76

# ANSWERING THE CALL

### Read 1 Samuel 3:1-18.

*"The Lord came and stood there, calling as at the other times, 'Samuel! Samuel!' Then Samuel said, 'Speak, for your servant is listening'" (v. 10).*

On a night when his team needed him, sophomore guard J.R. Reynolds answered the call, though he had to wait until he finished throwing up to do so.

The 8-2 Cavs were not at their best on Jan. 5, 2005, when they took on Western Kentucky. Forward Jason Clark was slowed by a strained Achilles tendon, and leading scorer Devin Smith missed the game with a severe ankle sprain. Plus, Reynolds shot a little before the game and then disappeared. He didn't go too far -- just into the bathroom to throw up. Repeatedly.

Apparently suffering from a rather nasty dose of food poisoning, Reynolds didn't appear on the floor again until the game was well under way. Then he was in front of the UVa bench having a bandage applied to his right arm, which had been bloodied by the two IVs he had received before the game.

Reynolds managed to play eight minutes in the first half but was way off his game. Intermission was not exactly a picnic for him. "He was throwing up at halftime," recounted head coach Pete Gillen. "We were talking as coaches and you could hear him. The poor kid was throwing up. We didn't think he could play."

So Gillen elected not to put Reynolds on the court as the last half began. Finally, the coach had no choice. As Western Kentucky kept a lead, Gillen looked over to Reynolds and asked him, "Can you play? Can you play?" Gillen's response was a simple, "Yes." Still, Gillen asked, "Are you sure?"

Reynolds was. He went into the game with 10:59 left and the Cavs trailing 47-43. "This is the worst I've ever felt and played," he said after the game. Answering the call, Reynolds incredibly scored a team-high 20 points, played on through the second overtime, and led the Cavs to an 80-79 win.

A team player is someone who does whatever the coach calls upon him to do for the good of the team. Something quite similar occurs when God places a specific call upon a Christian's life.

This is much scarier, though, than playing despite being sick as J.R. Reynolds did. The way many folks understand it is that answering God's call means going into the ministry, packing the family up, and moving halfway around the world to some place where folks have never heard of air conditioning, fried chicken, paved roads, or the Cavaliers. Zambia. The Philippines. Buffalo.

Not for you, no thank you. And who can blame you?

But God usually calls folks to serve him where they are. In fact, God put you where you are right now, and he has a purpose in placing you there. Wherever you are, you are called to serve him.

*Ninety-eight out of 100 guys are not going to play. They're going to say, 'Coach, I'm sorry. I've got an upset stomach.'*
-- *UVa basketball coach Pete Gillen on J.R. Reynolds*

**God calls you to serve him right now
right where he has put you, wherever that is.**

DAY 77

# THE GREATEST

**Read Mark 9:33-37.**

*"If anyone wants to be first, he must be the very last, and the servant of all" (v. 35).*

I can give you eight million reasons why North Carolina will beat Virginia," declared ESPN's bombastic Lee Corso. It looked like he knew what he was talking about until the Cavs pulled off the greatest fourth-quarter comeback in school history.

The 6th-ranked Tar Heels (8-1) appeared headed toward a conference title and a big bowl when they dominated 24th-ranked Virginia (6-3) through the first three quarters on Nov. 16, 1996. They led by two touchdowns in the fourth quarter and took possession at the Cavalier 10 after an interception. It was looking downright ugly. "Today, we were down and just about out," said UVa co-captain Todd White about the situation.

But then came one of those plays that become an indelible part of any successful football program's legend and lore. On second down, true freshman Antwan Harris anticipated a slant pattern, stepped in front of the Carolina receiver, and had nothing but 95 yards of green in front of him. With 10:02 left, UVa trailed only 17-10 instead of 24-3.

Duly inspired, the Cavalier defense, which held the Heels to a season low of 165 yards for the game and had seven sacks, forced a punt after three plays. Quarterback Tim Sherman led the offense onto the field with 8:13 left.

This time the offense produced, twice converting fourth-down plays. Sherman scored on a 7-yard run with 3:07 left. The game was tied at 17.

But the Cavs weren't through. The defense forced another Carolina punt, and Sherman hit wide receiver Germane Crowell with a 41-yard bomb to the Heel 15 with 1:47 left. With 39 ticks on the clock, Rafael Garcia's successful field goal completed UVa's greatest-ever fourth-quarter comeback.

We all want to be the greatest. The goal for the Cavs and their fans every season is at least the conference championship. The competition at work is to be the most productive sales person on the staff or the Teacher of the Year. In other words, we define being the greatest in terms of the struggle for personal success. It's nothing new; Jesus' disciples saw greatness in the same way.

As Jesus illustrated, though, greatness in the Kingdom of God has nothing to do with the world's understanding of success. Rather, the greatest are those who channel their ambition toward the furtherance of Christ's kingdom through love and service, rather than their own advancement, which is a complete reversal of status and values as the world sees them.

After all, who could be greater than the person who has Jesus for a brother and God for a father? And that's every one of us.

*My goal was to be the greatest athlete that ever lived.*
*-- Babe Didrikson Zaharias*

**To be great for God has nothing to do
with personal advancement and everything to do
with the advancement of Christ's kingdom.**

DAY 78

# PRESSURE COOKER

**Read 1 Kings 18:16-40.**

*"Answer me, O Lord, answer me, so these people will know that you, O Lord, are God" (v. 37).*

This night was all about pressure. Pressure on a quarterback, pressure on a coach, pressure on a program." Heck, there was even pressure on the stadium lights.

And on Oct. 15, 2005, when the sold-out crowd at Scott Stadium could finally relax from the almost overwhelming pressure wrought by a fourth-quarter FSU comeback, the Cavs had a 26-21 upset of the nation's 4th-ranked team.

Virginia quarterback Marques Hagans felt the quite literal pressure most of all as the Seminole front four went after a Cavalier offensive line that was missing senior tackle Brad Butler and was getting a rusty D'Brickashaw Ferguson back onto the field after missing some playing time. In response to the pressure, Hagans "danced around sacks, lofted the ball over outstretched arms [and] found throwing lanes when it looked like there were none." The result was 306 yards and two touchdowns.

But the whole team felt the pressure. A loss would have left the Cavs 1-3 in the ACC with bowl hopes fading fast. Head coach Al Groh felt the pressure of needing a win over a top-five team to prove his own program could compete with the big boys. Apparently feeling the pressure also, a bank of stadium lights wigged out and caused a 10-minute delay in the start of the last half.

# CAVALIERS

Late in the first half, the Cavaliers got a field goal from Connor Hughes and a 16-yard TD pass from Hagans to Wali Lundy to lead 23-10 at intermission. Hughes' fourth field goal of the game started the last-half scoring and made it 26-10.

But then in the fourth quarter came what everybody expected: the pressure of an FSU comeback. Only when junior safety Tony Franklin nabbed an interception with 50 seconds left to play was the pressure finally turned off.

You live every day with pressure. As Elijah did so long ago, you lay it on the line with everybody watching. Your family, coworkers, or employees – they depend on you. You know the pressure of a deadline, of a job evaluation, of taking the risk of asking someone to go out with you, of driving in rush-hour traffic.

Help in dealing with daily pressure is readily available, and the only price you pay for it is your willingness to believe. God will give you the grace to persevere if you ask prayerfully.

And while you may need some convincing, the pressures of daily living are really small potatoes since they all will pass. The real pressure comes when you stare into the face of eternity because what you do with it is irrevocable and forever. You can handle that pressure easily enough by deciding for Jesus. Eternity is then taken care of; the pressure's off – forever.

*Pressure is for tires.*

*-- Charles Barkley*

**The greatest pressure you face in life concerns where you will spend eternity, which can be dealt with by deciding for Jesus.**

## DAY 79

# AMAZING!

### Read: Luke 4:31-36.

*"All the people were amazed and said to each other, 'What is this teaching? With authority and power he gives orders to evil spirits and they come out!'" (v. 36)*

That the Cavs rallied to win the game was unbelievable enough. What Bryant Stith did to make the comeback happen, though, passed over into the downright amazing.

Stith is one of UVA's all-time greats. He finished his career in 1992 as Virginia's all-time leading scorer and second leading rebounder. He was a three-time honorable mention All-America and the sixth Virginia men's basketball player to have his jersey number retired. He was said to be "arguably the greatest clutch performer to wear a Cavalier uniform since Jeff Lamp." On Jan. 26, 1991, his amazing game "made some of his previous heroics seem unimpressive in comparison."

The 18th-ranked Cavaliers were in deep trouble against Notre Dame. They trailed 60-51 with only 3:14 left when Stith began what can only be described as his rampage with a steal that resulted in two free throws. He kept UVa in the game as time grew short. When point guard John Crotty fouled out with 1:48 left, the Cavs still trailed 66-59. At that point, said Stith, "I wanted to be the one to take charge."

He did -- and how. Over the last 3:14 of the game, Stith scored an amazing 17 points. "I don't know how it's possible to shoot

# CAVALIERS

enough to score 17 points in that short a period of time," said Cavalier guard Doug Smith. "You never want to think you're out of a game, but this was unbelievable." After Stith's driving dunk with 11 seconds left cut the Irish lead to 67-66, he won the game with two free throws with seven seconds left.

Stith had scored every one of UVa's last 19 points.

The word *amazing* defines the limits of what you believe to be plausible or usual. The Grand Canyon, the birth of your children, those last-second Cavalier wins -- they're amazing! You've never seen anything like that before!

Some people in Galilee felt the same way when they encountered Jesus. Jesus amazed them with the authority of his teaching, and he wowed them with his power over spirit beings. People everywhere just couldn't quit talking about him.

It would have been amazing had they not been amazed. They were, after all, witnesses to the most amazing spectacle in the history of the world: God himself was right there among them walking, talking, teaching, preaching, and healing.

Their amazement should be yours also because Jesus still lives. The almighty and omnipotent God of the universe seeks to spend time with you every day – because he loves you. Amazing!

*It's amazing. Some of the greatest characteristics of being a winning football player are the same ones it's true of being a Christian man.*
*-- Bobby Bowden*

**Everything about God is amazing,**
**but perhaps most amazing of all is that**
**he loves us and desires our company.**

# TRAGEDY

**Read Job 1; 2:1-10.**

*"In all this, Job did not sin by charging God with wrongdoing" (v. 1:22).*

The greatest tragedy in the history of the UVa football program changed the college game forever and ultimately helped save it.

On Nov. 13, 1909, in a game against Georgetown University, 18-year-old freshman halfback Archer Christian kicked a field goal and scored a touchdown to help put Virginia up 21-0. With about five minutes left to play, he plunged into the line as he had before; this time, though, Christian didn't get up. Barely conscious, he was taken to the sidelines. "Oh, I'm suffering, Pop," he said to the trainer. "Please do something for me."

Moments later, Christian lapsed into a coma and was rushed to Georgetown Hospital. Doctors performed emergency brain surgery, but could not save him. He died of a massive brain hemorrhage with his parents by his side. The repercussions of the young star's death were felt nationwide as opponents of the game rose up in arms, calling for it to be banned on college campuses.

Though terribly upset by Christian's death, UVa President Edwin Alderman fought to save the game. He led the charge to reform it by changing the rules to make it a safer game. He teamed with Virginia athletic director Dr. William Lambeth, considered the "Father of Virginia Athletics," to study and experiment with various rules changes.

Thanks in large part to Alderman's foresight and efforts, college football was changed and saved from itself. The reforms included abolishing several particularly brutal plays and requiring seven players on the line of scrimmage. In the wake of its great tragedy, "the fact that the University of Virginia led the way in reform perhaps saved the sport of football and made it a better game."

While we may receive them in varying degrees, suffering and tragedy are par for life's course. What we do with tragedy when it strikes us – as the sad story of Archer Christian's death illustrates – determines to a great extent how we live the rest of our lives.

We can – in accordance with the bitter suggestion Job's wife offered -- "Curse God and die," or we can trust God and live. That is, we can plunge into endless despair or we can lean upon the power of a transcendent faith in an almighty God who offers us hope in our darkest hours.

We don't have to understand tragedy; we certainly don't have to like it or believe there's anything fair about it. What we must do in such times, however, is trust in God's all-powerful love for us and his promise that all things will work for good for those who love him.

In choosing a life of ongoing trust in God in the face of our suffering, we prevent the greatest tragedy of all: that of a soul being cast into hell.

*When youth dies for loyalty's sake, the hallowed memory of love abides.*
*-- Inscription on tribute to Archer Christian in UVa chapel*

**Tragedy can drive us into despair and death or**
**into the life-sustaining arms of almighty God.**

# UNEXPECTEDLY

**Read Matthew 24:36-51.**

*"No one knows about that day or hour, not even the
angels in heaven, nor the Son, but only the Father" (v. 36).*

**M**uch about the 1994 Virginia-Virginia Tech game turned out
to be totally unexpected.

First of all, there was the score. The Cavs went into the game
with a 7-2 record; Tech was pretty strong that year, too, with an
8-2 record at kickoff. The first half was about what everybody
expected: close with Virginia leading 19-13 at the break. The last
half was totally unexpected, though, as the Cavs turned the game
into a cakewalk, winning easily 42-23.

Also unexpected was the reason behind the rout: The Hokies
committed an incredible eight turnovers, including five interceptions. UVa defensive backs Percy Ellsworth and Joe Crocker
nabbed two each. One of Crocker's thefts was totally unexpected;
he was on his back when a deflected ball landed in his lap.

Unexpected also was the record-setting performance of Cavalier kicker Rafael Garcia, a one-time Spanish exchange student.
He had had such a bad week at practice that he figured his team
would punt in any situation rather than let him kick. He had not
made a field goal of more than 40 yards all season. But perhaps
inspired because his father was seeing him play for the first time,
he booted a 43-yarder in the first quarter and wound up the day a
perfect five-for-five on field goals, which set a new school mark.

# CAVALIERS

Unexpected -- and disappointing for the Cavs -- were the bowl destinations of the two teams when the season ended. For the second year in a row, the loser of the contest wound up with the better bowl situation. The Cavs wound up in the Independence Bowl and beat TCU 20-10, which was just fine. But the Hokies wound up with the much bigger payday, getting a Gator-Bowl invite and pulling in $1.5 million despite losing to Tennessee.

All in all, nothing about the '94 game went as expected.

We think we've got everything figured out and under control, and then something unexpected happens. About the only thing we can expect from life with any certainty is the unexpected.

God is that way too, suddenly showing up to remind us he's still around. A friend who calls and tells you he's praying for you, a hug from your child or grandchild, a lone lily that blooms in your yard -- unexpected moments when the divine comes crashing into our lives with such clarity that it takes our breath away and brings tears to our eyes.

But why shouldn't God do the unexpected? The only factor limiting what God can do in our lives is the paucity of our own faith. We should expect the unexpected from God, this same deity who caught everyone by surprise by unexpectedly coming to live among us as a man, and who will return when we least expect it.

*I saw our players do things that I never have seen in practice.*
*— Frank Beamer on the eight turnovers he didn't expect against UVa*

**God continually does the unexpected,**
**like showing up as Jesus,**
**who will return unexpectedly.**

# THE GOOD OLD DAYS

### Read Psalm 102.

*"My days vanish like smoke; . . . but you remain the same,
and your years will never end" (vv. 3, 27).*

**D**on't let Barbara Kelly catch you waxing poetic about the "good old days." She knows that for women's basketball at UVa, those old days weren't quite so good.

In 1971, Kelly was hired as the first director of women's sports. Her first task was to find some athletes, which she did by placing an ad in *The Cavalier Daily*. In 1973, basketball, field hockey, and tennis became varsity sports with a $27,000 budget and volunteer coaches. Kelly, however, couldn't find a basketball coach, so she landed the job by default. She had no staff and no secretary, so she found officials, planned transportation, arranged schedules, and washed the one uniform each player had. She did it all.

To give the program exposure in those early days, the women's game often preceded the men's, but the clock would run to keep the game from intruding on the men's schedule. The first time the men's team manager asked Kelly to get her team off the floor in the middle of an overtime period, she said, "Excuse me. You've got to be kidding" and told him to go do something that was extremely dangerous to his health.

The women had to practice at Memorial Gym and were often relegated to using a basket on one of the side courts. Not pleased with having to share the training facilities with the women, some male athletes walked around nude in the training room, figuring they'd drive the females away. The men's coach once locked up the gym, thus locking out the fans for the women's game that night. Told University Hall had no office space for her, Kelly searched the building until she found a storage room and converted it.

After two seasons, Kelly had had enough of coaching in the good old days, gave it up, and turned her attention to developing all of the women's sports.

It's a brutal truth that time just never stands still. The current of your life sweeps you along until you realize one day you've lived long enough to have a past. Part of it you cling to fondly. The stunts you pulled with your high-school buddies. Your first apartment. That dance with your first love. That special vacation. Those "good old days."

You hold on relentlessly to the memory of those old, familiar ways because of the stability they provide in our uncertain world. They will always be there even as times change and you age.

Another constant exists in your life too. God has been a part of every event in your life that created a memory because he was there. He's always there with you; the question is whether you ignore him or make him a part of your day.

A "good old day" is any day shared with God.

*Nobody had any respect for her at all. They treated her like dirt. And she would just come back every day and keep working away at it.*
*-- Dan Bonner on Barbara Kelly, whom he succeeded as women's coach*

**Today is one of the "good old days"**
**if you share it with God.**

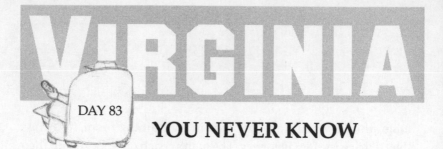

# YOU NEVER KNOW

**Read Exodus 3:1-12.**

*"But Moses said to God, 'Who am I, that I should go to Pharaoh and bring the Israelites out of Egypt?' And God said, 'I will be with you'" (vv. 11-12a).*

It didn't look like we had the kind of energy it was going to take to come back and win the ballgame." But you never know -- even if you are the head coach.

When UVa's Dave Leitao met his team in a time out on Jan. 28, 2007, with less than twelve minutes to play, the Cavs trailed 19th-ranked Clemson 52-41. The coach looked over his team and didn't like what he saw, eliciting his post-game comment about the lack of energy.

But that bunch that Leitao feared didn't have enough energy went out and pulled off one of the most remarkable comebacks in UVa basketball history. Nothing Leitao saw at first changed his mind. Instead, the 11-point lead went to 14 at 63-49 with only 5:05 on the clock, but the Tigers would not score another point. Proving once again that even a head coach who knows the game of basketball never knows about a particular game, the Cavs scored 15 straight points and won 64-63.

Adrian Joseph scored eight points, and senior J.R. Reynolds added five to key the comeback. Reynolds finished the night with a game-high 18 points. But it was All-ACC point guard Sean Singletary who made the big play that gave the Cavs a chance to win it. They trailed by one when Singletary snared an offensive rebound and passed to Joseph with 20 seconds left. Joseph missed a shot, but Jason Cain tipped in the game-winner with 17 seconds to play. Clemson's last-ditch shot for a win went over the basket.

"I'm not sure if I've ever seen a game like this before," Leitao said. Hey, coach, you just never know.

You never know what you can do until – like the Cavs against Clemson -- you want to bad enough or until – like Moses -- you have to. Serving in the military, maybe even in combat. Standing by a friend while everyone else unjustly excoriates her. Playing a new game at the collegiate level. Undergoing agonizing medical treatment and managing to smile. You never know what life will demand of you.

It's that way too in your relationship with God. As Moses discovered, you never know where or when God will call you or what God will ask of you. You do know that God expects you to be faithful and willing to trust him even when he calls you to tasks that daunt and dismay you.

You can respond faithfully to whatever God calls you to do for him. That's because even though you never know what lies ahead, you do know that God will both lead you and provide what you need.

*There's one word to describe baseball: You never know.*
*– Yogi Berra*

**You never know what God will ask you to do,**
**but you always know he will provide everything**
**you need to do it.**

# VIRGINIA

## GLORY DAYS

### Read Colossians 3:1-4.

*"When Christ, who is your life, appears, then you also will appear with him in glory" (v. 4).*

Anthony Poindexter gets to relive the most glorious of his glory days all the time.

That's because rarely a week goes by -- more than a decade after it happened -- that UVa fans don't approach him on the street, in the grocery store, in a restaurant, or about anywhere else he happens to be and ask him about "the Florida State play."

Poindexter is one of the greatest players in Cavalier football history. He was a first-team All-American safety both his junior and senior seasons (1997-98). As a senior, he was the ACC Defensive Player of the Year and is only one of three players in UVa history to be first-team All-ACC three times. He had so many glorious days as a Cavalier football player that his jersey number was retired in 2009.

One day, though, stands out above them all. On Nov. 2, 1995, as a freshman, he helped make what has been called "perhaps the biggest single defensive play in school history": the Florida State play. Virginia held a slim 33-28 lead, but the 2nd-ranked Seminoles had one last play just outside the Cavalier goal line. The Noles snapped the ball directly to tailback Warrick Dunn in the shotgun formation. Linebacker Skeet Jones saw the play coming and started screaming directions to his teammates even

as Dunn took the snap and streaked toward the goal line.

Linebacker Jamie Sharper got a hand on a Dunn ankle and slowed him as he staggered forward. Only inches from the goal line, Poindexter and fellow safety Adrian Burnim stopped Dunn.

UVa's upset that glorious day was FSU's first-ever loss in ACC play, ending a 29-game streak that stretched back to 1992.

You may well remember the play that was your moment of athletic glory. Or the night you received an award from a civic group for your hard work. Your first (and last?) ace on the golf course. Your promotion at work. Your first-ever 10K race. Life does have its moments of glory.

But they amount to a lesser, transient glory, which bears pain with it since you cannot recapture the moment. The excitement, the joy, even the happiness – they are fleeting; they pass as quickly as they arose, and you can never experience them again.

Glory days that last forever are found only through Jesus. That's because true glory properly belongs only to God, who has shown us his glory in Jesus. To accept Jesus into our lives is thus to take God's glory into ourselves. Glory therefore is an ongoing attribute of Christians. Our glory days are right now, and they will become even more glorious when Jesus returns.

*I know he didn't. If I thought he got in, I wouldn't have jumped up in the air like I did.*
*-- Anthony Poindexter on Warrick Dunn's claim that he scored*

**The glory of this earth is fleeting,**
**but the glory we find in Jesus lasts forever**
**– and will only get even more magnificent.**

# OLD-FASHIONED FOLKS

**Read Leviticus 18:1-5.**

*"You must obey my laws and be careful to follow my decrees. I am the Lord your God" (v. 4).*

The UVa football team didn't cheer, shout, or jump up and down when they received some momentous news. They knew what the school's old-fashioned response would be.

Coach Art Guepe's Cavaliers of 1951 went 8-1 with wins over Virginia Tech (33-0), Duke, North Carolina, and South Carolina. They finished the regular season ranked no. 13 in the nation. The squad's only loss came to a powerhouse Washington & Lee team, a defeat that All-American defensive guard Joe Palumbo said happened because "frankly, we just took them too lightly."

Palumbo was the Cavaliers' star that season, a first-team All-America who later became the sixth Virginia player to have his jersey number retired. In 1999, he was inducted into the National Football Foundation and the College Football halls of fame.

He wrapped up his storied collegiate career on Nov. 24, 1951, with a 46-0 thrashing of William & Mary. In the locker room after the game, he gathered with his teammates around Guepe. As usual, the coach was brief and to the point. "Gentlemen," he said. "I want to congratulate you on a fine game. I just met with the folks from the Cotton Bowl, and they want us to come to Dallas."

That announcement should have set off a raucous celebration. No Virginia football team had ever been to a bowl game, and here was one of the biggies -- a New Year's Day game -- inviting them. But there was no outburst, and the reason was simple. "We knew we weren't going anywhere," Palumbo said.

He was right. Within hours, the university's president turned down the invitation. His old-fashioned reason? "We don't want to go professional," he said.

Usually, when we refer to some person, some idea, or some institution as old-fashioned, we deliver a full-fledged or at least thinly veiled insult. They're out of step with the times and the mores, hopelessly out of date, totally irrelevant, and quite useless.

For the people of God, however, "old-fashioned" is exactly the lifestyle we should pursue. The throwbacks are the ones who value honor, dignity, sacrifice, and steadfastness, who can be counted on to tell the truth and to do what they say. Old-fashioned folks shape their lives according to eternal values and truths, the ones handed down by almighty God.

These ancient laws and decrees are still relevant to contemporary life because they direct us to a lifestyle of holiness and righteousness that serves us well every single day. Such a way of living allows us to escape the ultimately hopeless life to which so many have doomed themselves in the name of being modern.

*We felt pretty honored, but we didn't expect to go. There was not a thing we could do about it. Except to forget it.*
*-- Joe Palumbo on UVa's rejection of the Cotton Bowl invitation*

**The ancient lifestyle God calls us to still leads us to a life of contentment, peace, and joy, which never grows old-fashioned.**

# VIRGINIA

## DAY 86

# THE PIONEER SPIRIT

**Read Luke 5:1-11.**

*"So they pulled their boats up on shore, left everything and followed him" (v. 11).*

Typically, colleges look back to the early 1970s for the pioneers and trailblazers in their women's sports. Not UVa. Virginia had a female athlete earn a varsity letter in the 1950s.

In the spring of 1971, the university announced an ambitious plan to expand opportunities for its female athletes The first women's club teams -- tennis, field hockey, and basketball -- began competition that fall. They received varsity status for the 1973-74 school year. The first female athlete to receive an athletic scholarship at UVa was long-distance runner Margaret Groos. In 1981, she set a world record in the indoor 5,000 meter run. Five of her school records still stand. She graduated from UVa in 1982 and went on to win the marathon in the 1988 Olympic trials.

These women certainly blazed a trail for others to follow that eventually led to the success and the popularity that women's college sports enjoys today. But they were not the first in Charlottesville. Shoot, they weren't even close.

In 1953, Mary Slaughter arrived at the university seeking a master's degree in education. She was no stranger to Cavalier athletics. Her father was Edward R. "Butch" Slaughter, who had a lengthy UVa career coaching football, baseball, and golf and directing the school's intramural program.

# CAVALIERS

She well knew that no opportunities existed for her to play college tennis -- so she made one. In 1954, she joined the men's tennis team. While at UVa, she won the Women's Eastern Intercollegiate championship.

Thus, two decades before the official launch of women's athletics at Virginia, Mary Slaughter was the first female Cavalier to play a varsity sport and the first to earn a varsity letter.

Going to a place in your life you've never been before requires a willingness to take risks and face uncertainty head-on. You may have never been a sports pioneer at a major college, but you've had your moments when your latent pioneer spirit manifested itself. That time you changed careers, ran a marathon, volunteered at a homeless shelter, learned Spanish, or went back to school.

While attempting new things invariably begets apprehension, the truth is that when life becomes too comfortable and too familiar, it gets boring. The same is true of God, who is downright dangerous because he calls us to be anything but comfortable as we serve him. He summons us to continuously blaze new trails in our faith life, to follow him no matter what. Stepping out on faith is risky all right, but the reward is a life of accomplishment, adventure, and joy that cannot be equaled anywhere else.

*Life is an adventure. I wouldn't want to know what's going to happen next.*

*-- Bobby Bowden*

**Unsafe and downright dangerous, God calls us out of the place where we are comfortable to a life of adventure and trailblazing in his name.**

# IN THE BAD TIMES

### Read Philippians 1:3-14.

*"What has happened to me has really served to advance
the gospel. . . . Because of my chains, most of the brothers
in the Lord have been encouraged to speak the word of
God more courageously and fearlessly" (vv. 12, 14).*

Times were once so bad at UVa that when a football coach told
his team in the locker room before a game that they were going to
win, they laughed at him.

The 1951 football season opened amid the dropping of a bomb-
shell with the appearance of the "Gooch Report," which bore the
name of Bobby Gooch, a professor of political science and the
quarterback of the 8-1 team of 1914. The report recommended that
the awarding of athletic scholarships at UVa be discontinued and
expressed a preference that football be dropped. While neither
drastic step was taken, of course, a study released later in the
decade revealed that while its ACC brethren kept between 80 and
125 scholarshipped football players on hand, UVa typically had
only about 35.

The resulting bad times were predictable. As the 1961 season
opened, the Cavs had tied an all-time collegiate record by losing
28 straight games. After two straight winless seasons, UVa hired
young Bill Elias to win some games. "They say it can't be done
here," the new coach said. "Like the idiot I am, I think I'll try it."

Elias' first game was against William & Mary. He recalled, "In the dressing room before we went out on the field that day, I said to the team, 'You may not believe this, but you're going to come off the field a winner today.' All of them burst into laughter."

So much for an inspiring pre-game talk. But Elias was right. The Cavs won 21-6, the fans tore down the goal posts and gave Elias a victory ride, and UPI named him its National Coach of the Week. For one day at least, the bad times were gone.

Loved ones die. You're downsized. Your biopsy looks cancerous. Your spouse could be having an affair. Hard, tragic times are as much a part of life as breath.

This applies to Christians too. Christianity is not the equivalent of a Get-out-of-Jail-Free card, granting us a lifelong exemption from either the least or the worst pain the world has to offer. While Jesus promises us he will be there to lead us through the valleys, he never promises that we will not enter them.

The question therefore becomes how you handle the bad times You can fall to your knees in despair and cry, "Why me?" Or you can hit your knees in prayer and ask, "What do I do with this?"

Setbacks and tragedies are opportunities to reveal and to develop true character and abiding faith. Your faithfulness -- not your skipping merrily along through life without pain -- is what reveals the depth of your love for God.

*If I were to say, "God, why me?" about the bad things, then I should say, "God, why me?" about the good things that happen in my life.*
*-- Arthur Ashe*

**Faithfulness to God requires faith even in --**
**especially in -- the bad times.**

# VIRGINIA

# LANGUAGE BARRIER

### Read Acts 2:1-21.

*"Divided tongues, as of fire, appeared among them, and a tongue rested on each of them. All of them were filled with the Holy Spirit and began to speak in other languages, as the Spirit gave them ability" (vv. 3-4 NRSV).*

Football has its own peculiar and arcane language, especially when it comes to play-calling. Against Clemson in 1995, the 11th-ranked Cavs suffered a communications breakdown on one play -- and the result was a touchdown.

Cavalier head coach George Welsh knew it was going to be a good weekend when his room assignment at the hotel was 711. "We couldn't lose, could we?" he joked about the combination of "lucky" numbers. The Cavs may have needed a little luck since they went into the game 0-17-1 in Death Valley. As it turned out, they actually got a little luck when one of the contest's biggest plays resulted from a language problem.

The Cavaliers led 12-3 in the third quarter and faced third-and-14 at their own 24. The coaches sent wide receiver Patrick Jeffers in with the play, and he showed up "yelling a jumble of letters and numbers that said [quarterback Mike] Groh was supposed to throw him a slant pass underneath the Tigers' coverage."

Apparently, though, Jeffers "mix[ed] up his ABC's and 123's." As the play unfolded, Groh waited for Jeffers to come underneath, but instead, the receiver gave a defensive back a fake and took off down the sideline. Finally, to avoid a sack, Groh double-pumped and threw the ball up. He hit Jeffers almost in stride for a 76-yard touchdown that blew the game open.

The Cavs went on to win 22-3, their victory clinched on a play with a language problem.

As the touchdown play against Clemson illustrates, language often erects a barrier to understanding. Recall your overseas vacation or your call to a tech support number when you got someone who spoke English but didn't understand it. Talking loud and waving your hands doesn't facilitate communication; it just makes you look weird.

Like many other aspects of life, faith has its jargon that can sometimes hinder understanding. Sanctification, justification, salvation, Advent, Communion with its symbolism of eating flesh and drinking blood – these and many other words have specific meanings to Christians that may be incomprehensible, confusing, and downright daunting to the newcomer or the seeker.

But the heart of Christianity's message centers on words that require no explanation: words such as hope, joy, love, purpose, and community. Their meanings are universal because people the world over seek them in their lives. Nobody speaks that language better than Jesus.

*There was a miscommunication in the huddle.*
*-- Patrick Jeffers on the 76-yard touchdown play against Clemson*

**Jesus speaks across all language barriers
because his message of hope and meaning
resounds with people everywhere.**

DAY 89

# TOP SECRET

### Read Romans 2:1-16.

*"This will take place on the day when God will judge men's secrets through Jesus Christ, as my gospel declares"* *(v. 16).*

**W**hen she was a senior at UVa, Dena Evans carried around a secret that became a precious souvenir of her time as a Cavalier.

Standing only 5'4", Evans was named the best point in the nation and the country's best player under 5'7" as a senior in 1993. The '93 Cavs won 21 games in the regular season and won the ACC regular and tournament championships. In that tourney final against Maryland, which went into three overtimes, both Heather and Heidi Burge fouled out and Wendy Palmer suffered an injury, leaving Evans to put the team on her back.

She played all 55 minutes, hit a trey with 12 seconds left to tie the game in regulation, and then nailed a game-tying baseline jumper in the closing seconds of the first overtime. Evans scored 19 points, and after the 106-103 UVa win, she was named the tournament MVP. In an interesting twist, she was only second-team All-Tournament because of when the ballots were sent in.

It has been said of Evans that she "probably worked harder than anyone else in her four years in Charlottesville." She described herself as a gym rat who often wheedled, begged, and coerced the University Hall night watchman into letting her secretly into the building at night so she could shoot. One night during her senior year, men's basketball assistant Dennis Wolff was preparing to lock up when Evans showed up. He said, "I don't know anybody who deserves this and would get more use out of this than you." And he handed her a key to U Hall.

The key was a precious secret Evans told nobody about because "I didn't want anybody to take it away from me." Years afterward, she still had the secret key, which she called "sacred."

We all have secrets and information that we prefer to keep from others. Despite our best efforts, much information about us -- from credit reports to what movies we rent -- is readily available to prying and persistent persons. In our information age, people we don't know may know a lot about us — or at least they can find out. And some of them may use this information for harm.

While diligence may allow us to be reasonably successful in keeping some secrets from the world at large, we should never deceive ourselves into believing we are keeping secrets from God. God knows everything about us, including the things we wouldn't want proclaimed at church. All our sins, mistakes, failures, short-comings, quirks, prejudices, and desires – God knows all our would-be secrets.

But here's something God hasn't kept a secret: No matter what he knows about us, he loves us still.

*I have a lot of good memories of being in there, kind of shooting and dreaming and the lights being real low, and the gym being empty.*
*— Dena Evans on her secret late-night trips to U Hall*

**We have no secrets before God, and it's no secret that he nevertheless loves us still.**

## DAY 90

# RESPECTFULLY YOURS

**Read Mark 8:31-38.**

*"He then began to teach them that the Son of Man must suffer many things and be rejected by the elders, chief priests and teachers of the law, and that he must be killed"* (v. 31).

In perhaps the greatest show of respect by an opposing team in Virginia football history, the North Carolina Tar Heels in 1941 helped the Wahoos carry a Virginia football legend off the field in celebration of the great game he had against them.

When the powers-that-be hired Frank Murray in 1937 to head up Virginia's struggling football program, they brought in a rather unorthodox coach. For instance, he sought to reverse a series of losses to VPI by having his team practice at midnight the week of the game. "The Cavaliers stumbled about the field with only illuminated tape on the ball to light their way." He also broke out new uniforms for the game that were allegedly "bought for their ability to withstand hard knocks."

But Murray could coach -- and recruit. On a recruiting trip, he found "a skinny little back with average speed, a mediocre arm, and an awkward kicking style." What he found was a football legend named William "Bullet Bill" Dudley.

As a junior halfback in 1940, he led the Southern Conference in total offense. As a senior, he was Virginia's first-ever All America and won the Maxwell Award as the nation's best college football

player. He led the nation in touchdowns, points scored, and rushing average and was the first overall pick in the NFL draft.

In the 1941 win over North Carolina (28-7), Dudley rushed 17 times for 215 yards, scored three touchdowns on runs of 67, 69, and three yards, completed six of 11 passes for 117 yards, punted eight times, and starred at safety. When Dudley came to the bench late in the game, the UNC crowd gave him a standing ovation. The Tar Heel players likewise showed their respect for Dudley by helping his teammates carry him off the field to the locker room.

Rodney Dangerfield made a good living as a comedian with a repertoire that was basically only countless variations on one punch line: "I don't get no respect." Dangerfield was successful because he struck a chord with his audience. Everyone wants to be a respected by his peers. You want the respect, the esteem, and the regard that you feel you've earned.

But more often than not, you don't get it. Still, you shouldn't feel too badly; you're in good company. In the ultimate example of disrespect, Jesus – the very Son of God -- was treated as the worst type of criminal. He was arrested, bound, scorned, ridiculed, spit upon, tortured, condemned, and executed.

God allowed his son to undergo such treatment because of his high regard and his love for you. You are respected by almighty God! Could anyone else's respect really matter?

*Play for your own self-respect and the respect of your teammates.*
*-- Legendary Vanderbilt coach Dan McGugin*

**You may not get the respect you deserve,**
**but at least nobody's spitting on you**
**and driving nails into you as they did to Jesus.**

### DAY 91

# BELIEVE IT

**Read John 3:16-21.**

*"For God so loved the world that He gave His only begotten Son, that whoever believes in Him should not perish but have everlasting life" (v. 16 NKJV).*

How bad was it? The band played "Don't Stop Believing." The players knew that practically nobody believed they could win. Fearing nasty content, administrators for a while banned signs from the game. Believers in the Cavaliers were hard to find.

The experts, the pundits, and probably many of the Cavalier fans just didn't believe Virginia had much of a chance against Maryland on Oct. 4, 2008. They had their reasons. The 4-1 Terrapins sashayed into Scott Stadium on a three-game win streak that included wins over Clemson and California, both ranked in the top 25 at the time.

The Cavs, on the other hand, were not doing too well. They were 1-3, had been outscored 128-20 by their three major foes, and were 119th among the 119 major teams in total offense. They had yet to throw a single touchdown pass. "Everybody made it seem like we were the worst team in America," said linebacker Clint Sintim. Even the band took notice of the Cavs' woes, ending its halftime show with Journey's "Don't Stop Believing" as if anything, even a UVa win over Maryland, were possible.

Turned out it was. The fans streaming toward the exits before the game was over weren't UVa followers; they were Maryland fans who had seen more than enough. Virginia simply slaughtered Maryland 31-0.

Sophomore quarterback Marc Verica threw two TD passes and ran for another as the Cavs jumped out to a 21-0 halftime lead. Cedric Peerman's 9-yard scoring run made it 31-0 with 5:21 left in the third quarter.

Cavalier fans started believing again.

What we believe underscores everything about our lives. Our politics. How we raise our children. How we treat other people. Whether we respect others, their property and their lives.

Often, competing belief systems clamor for our attention; we all know persons – maybe friends and family members – who have lost Christianity in the shuffle and the hubbub. We turn aside from believing in Christ at our peril, however, because the heart and soul, the very essence of Christianity, is belief. That is, believing that Jesus is the very Son of God and that it is through him – and only through him – that we can find forgiveness and salvation that will reserve a place for us with God.

But believing is more than simply acknowledging intellectually that Jesus is God. Even the demons who serve Satan know that. It is belief so deep that we entrust our lives and our eternity to Christ. We live like we believe it – because we do.

*Honestly, I don't think there were too many people in this world who thought we were going to win this game.*

*-- UVa linebacker Clint Sintim*

**Believe it: Jesus is the way – and the only way
– to eternal life with God.**

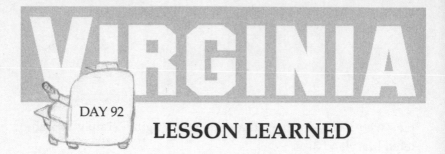

DAY 92

# LESSON LEARNED

**Read Psalm 143.**

*"Teach me to do your will, for you are my God" (v. 10).*

**K**evin Arico had to learn a valuable lesson before he could be-come a vital cog in the best two-year run in UVa baseball history.

The diamond Cavaliers of 2009 and 2010 won an astounding 100 games. The '09 squad set a school record with 49 wins, but that victory total was eclipsed by the 51 wins of the 2010 team.

Arico was pivotal to that success. As the closer both seasons, he saved a combined 29 games, second only in school history to Casey Lambert's 43 saves from 2004-07. As a sophomore in 2009, Arico was second in the ACC with 11 saves. In 2010, his 18 saves was a school record, tied the ACC season record, and led the nation. He was a first-team All-ACC selection with a 2.88 ERA.

But Arico didn't start out as a closer. Standing 6-foot-4, he was an imposing presence on the mound as a starter in high school. When he came to UVa, head coach Brian O'Connor made a relief pitcher out of him. He was 2-0 with a 5.02 ERA as a freshman.

Early in the 2009 season, O'Connor figured Arico had what it took to be a closer. "Not only is his stuff really good," O'Conner said about his decision, but "he's got great poise. He does not believe that anybody can beat him."

The change was hard. "Going into it, it was very difficult for me," Arico said. "At first I struggled with it." What he found most troublesome was that when he came into a game now, a win or a loss was usually on the line. So he learned a lesson every closer has to: "Having a short-term memory is critical. It takes time and it's a big adjustment, but it's something you have to learn."

Arico demonstrated the value of that lesson against Ole Miss in the championship of the Super Regional. He gave up a walk-off home run that lost the first game, but put it behind him and came back to retire three straight Rebel batters in the deciding game. The Cavs were on their way to the College World Series.

Learning about anything in life requires a combination of education and experience. Education is the accumulation of facts that we call knowledge; experience is the acquisition of wisdom and discernment, which add purpose and understanding to our knowledge.

The most difficult way to learn is trial and error: dive in blindly and mess up. The best way to learn is through example coupled with a set of instructions: Someone goes ahead to show you the way and writes down all the information you need to follow.

In teaching us the way to live godly lives, God chose the latter method. He set down in his book the habits, actions, and attitudes that make for a way of life in accordance with his wishes. He also sent us Jesus to explain and to illustrate.

God teaches us not just how to exist but how to live. We just need to be attentive students.

*It's important to flush it out [of your mind] and go after the next hitter.*
*— Kevin Arico on having a short-term memory as a closer*

**To learn from Jesus is to learn what life is all about and how God means for us to live it.**

## DAY 93

# PROVE IT

### Read Matthew 3.

*"But John tried to deter him, saying, 'I need to be baptized by you, and do you come to me?'" (v. 14)*

The Cavaliers were so intent on proving themselves that they willingly and shamelessly stole their opening-game opponent's motto and used it for their own inspiration.

UVa opened the 1998 football season on Sept. 4 against Auburn on the road. The preseason polls had the Cavs ranked No. 16 and Auburn at No. 25. The Tigers' head coach, Terry Bowden, was so miffed by his team's "low" ranking that he came up with a mantra: "STP." It had nothing to do with a well-known fuel additive and everything to do with "Something to Prove."

The Cavs felt it nailed their own attitude about the game, that they had something to prove themselves. For one thing, UVa had lost its last five games and six of its last seven match-ups against ranked opponents. For another, Auburn had whipped them 28-17 in the 1997 season opener. However wrong, the perception was that the Cavs couldn't beat a really good team on the road.

Forget that. UVa went out and humiliated Auburn 19-0, the first time since 1927 the Tigers had been shut out in their home opener. "We got to hush our critics tonight," declared All-American free safety Anthony Poindexter.

The defeat of a team that had won 20 straight regular-season, non-conference games may have been even easier than the 19-0

# CAVALIERS

score indicated. Auburn crossed midfield only once and never got inside the Cavs' 46-yard line the second half. Only 26 of Auburn's 53 plays gained yardage. The Virginia defense held the Tigers to -5 yards rushing in the second half and 18 for the game.

On this one night, the Cavaliers did all the proving.

You, too, have to prove yourself over and over again in your life. To your teachers, to that guy you'd like to date, to your parents, to your bosses, to the loan officer. It's always the same question: "Am I good enough?" Practically everything we do in life is aimed at proving that we are.

And yet, when it comes down to the most crucial situation in our lives, the answer is always a decisive and resounding "No!" Are we good enough to measure up to God? To deserve our salvation? John the Baptist knew he wasn't, and he was not only Jesus' relative but God's hand-chosen prophet. If he wasn't good enough, what chance do we have?

The notion that only "good" people can be church members is a perversion of Jesus' entire ministry. Nobody is good enough – without Jesus. Everybody is good enough – with Jesus. That's not because of anything we have done for God, but because of what he has done for us. We have nothing to prove to God.

*I don't want to be stealing their motto, but in the back of my mind, I thought we had something to prove, too.*
*-- UVa safety Anthony Poindexter*

**The bad news is we can't prove to God how good we are; the good news is that because of Jesus we don't have to.**

# GRAND ENTRANCE

**Read Luke 2:1-20.**

*"She gave birth to her firstborn, a son. She wrapped him in cloths and placed him in a manger, because there was no room for them in the inn" (v. 7).*

The ACC Tournament didn't exactly make a grand entrance in 1954, but UVa's Buzzy Wilkinson sure did.

Today, of course, the league's postseason tournament is the biggest show in college basketball short of the NCAA's annual soiree. But the fledgling conference was only six months old with seven charter members when it held its first throwdown in 1954.

That first tournament was played in Raleigh even though NC State was ineligible for the NCAA Tournament berth that went to the winner. State was allowed to play, according to sports editor Bill Brill, because "If State hadn't been playing, there wouldn't have been anybody in the stands."

Like many fans, area papers pretty much regarded the tournament with indifference. Very few papers even sent a reporter to Raleigh. One morning during the tournament, the lead basketball story of *The Roanoke Times* was West Virginia's win over Washington and Lee in the Southern Conference Tournament.

That didn't keep Wilkinson from making a splashy entrance, though. He remains one of the greatest and most overlooked players in UVa history, his career average of 32.1 points per game still the ACC record. He was the first Virginia player to have his

CAVALIERS

jersey retired and was drafted by the Boston Celtics.

The 16-10 Cavs drew top-seeded Duke for their first-ever ACC Tournament game. They were destroyed 96-68, but Wilkinson hoisted 44 shots, a tournament record for shot attempts that still stands. He scored 42 points, second in tourney history only to the 45 put up by UNC's Len Rosenbluth in 1957.

A splashy grand entrance is certainly a crowd pleaser. Entertainment reporters breathlessly prowl the red carpet at awards shows to gush over the starlets who have carefully chosen a wardrobe designed for maximum effect and attention. The U.S. president strides into view while a band plays "Hail to the Chief." Music erupts and the crowd sends up a deafening roar when the Cavaliers trot onto the field at Scott Stadium before a game.

And then there's Jesus. Being God, he could have made the grandest entrance of all, riding down from the heavens in a fiery chariot and coming as a full-grown warrior full of wrath, fury, and righteous indignation. Instead, he entered this world relatively unnoticed, as a helpless baby tended by a teenaged peasant mother and watched over by some livestock.

He will return, though, and next time he will make the grandest entrance of them all. He will come as the King of Kings to claim his kingdom. We had all better be ready to welcome him.

*You better stop shooting or you're going to ruin your reputation.*
*-- UVa coach Bus Male to Buzzy Wilkinson on his poor shooting night*
*in the ACC Tournament*

**Jesus has made one less-than-grand entrance; the next time he shows up will be entirely different.**

DAY 95

# THE GREAT CELEBRATION

### Read Luke 15:1-10.

*"There is rejoicing in the presence of the angels of God over one sinner who repents" (v. 10).*

UVa's win over Penn in 1949 touched off celebrations in two states, one so rowdy that Philadelphia's hotel association adopted a policy forbidding the acceptance in the future of reservations for anyone from the state of Virginia.

The time immediately after World War II was a golden era for Cavalier football. Veterans came home and took advantage of the G.I. Bill to go to college, especially at Virginia where 40 of the 47 players on the 1946 football team were vets.

The veterans of 1949 pulled off a monumental upset of an East-Coast powerhouse reminiscent of the 1915 team's win over Yale. (See Devotion No. 75.) UVa and Penn had played fourteen times since 1890, and Virginia had never won. The 20th-ranked Quakers weren't supposed to lose in '49 either, playing at home in Phila-delphia before almost 51,000 spectators that included a small but apparently very lively contingent of Cavalier fans.

Virginia simply took it to Penn. Halfback Steve Osisek rushed for one touchdown, passed for another, and caught seven passes for 100 yards. Virginia led 17-0 in the first half and won 26-14.

The big win touched off a wild celebration by Virginia's fans in Philly, and they apparently got more than a little carried away. The Philadelphia Hotel Association claimed that "Virginians

# CAVALIERS

ran through the hallways all hours of the night, smashing signs, throwing beer and harassing elevator operators." In response to the celebration, the association declared that its member hotels would no longer accept any reservations for folks from Virginia.

When the team returned home, 7,000 horn-tooting, celebrating fans and the mayor escorted them in open cars back to campus. One car boasted a flag that had been part of a Penn goal post.

UVa just whipped Virginia Tech. You got that new job or that promotion. You just held your newborn child in your arms. Life has those grand moments that call for celebration. You may jump up and down and scream in a wild frenzy at Scott Stadium or share a quiet, sedate candlelight dinner at home -- but you celebrate.

Consider then a celebration that is beyond our imagining, one that reverberates through every niche and every corner of the very household of God and the angels. Imagine a celebration in Heaven, which also has its grand moments.

Those unimaginable celebrations at God's place are touched off when someone comes to faith in Jesus. Heaven itself rings with the joyous sounds of the singing and dancing of the celebrating angels. Even God rejoices when just one person – you or someone you have introduced to Christ? -- turns to him.

When you said "yes" to Christ, you made the angels dance.

*When it comes to celebrating, act like you've been there before.*
*-- Terry Bowden*

**God himself joins the angels**
**in heavenly celebration when even a**
**single person turns to him through faith in Jesus.**

## DAY 96

# WEATHERPROOFED

### Read Nahum 1:3-9.

*"His way is in the whirlwind and the storm, and clouds are the dust of his feet" (v. 3b).*

In Virginia's first-ever trip to the soccer national championship game, neither team won. The weather did.

The 1989 final four was played at Rutgers. Semifinal Saturday on Dec. 2 was clear and cold with subzero wind chills and a few flakes of snow. The weather seemed not to bother the Cavs, who blitzed the hosts 3-0 to set up the title game against Santa Clara.

The weather may have been only an inconvenience on Saturday, but it was the determining factor in the title game the next day. Where the field wasn't covered with ice, it was frozen, and the players struggled to gain any traction. Temperatures dropped into the teens, pushing the wind chills to -30. Santa Clara's Paul Bravo said, "Halfway through the first half, my face was pretty much frozen. I couldn't get up enough energy to scream."

The Cavs broke out first when Lyle Yorks delivered a corner kick to Richie Williams, who headed the ball across to Drew Fallon, who scored from six yards out. Late in the last half, Santa Clara tied the game at 1. The teams thus headed into overtime.

The problem was that because of the weather, the two teams "could have played forever . . . and nobody would have scored." Some players couldn't feel their feet on the ball, making dribbling upfield virtually impossible. The cold affected the ball, making it difficult to kick it more than twenty yards. "Overtime was cruel and unusual punishment," but the teams played 60 minutes of it before being declared co-champions. The weather had won out.

Realizing the conditions had rendered the title game a "theater of the absurd," the NCAA the next season put the finals up for bid and selected a site in sunny, warm Florida.

A thunderstorm washes away your golf game or the picnic with the kids. Lightning knocks out the electricity just as you settle in at the computer. A tornado interrupts your Sunday dinner and sends everyone scurrying to the hallway. A hurricane cancels your beach trip.

For all our technology and our knowledge, we are still at the mercy of the weather, able only to get a little more advance warning than in the past. The weather answers only to God. Cold temperatures are totally inconsiderate of something as important as a Cavalier soccer match or football game.

We stand mute before the awesome power of the weather, but we should be even more awestruck at the power of the one who controls it, a power beyond our imagining. Neither, however, can we imagine the depths of God's love for us, a love that drove him to die on a cross for us.

*The conditions were such that it wasn't fair for the players to be out there anymore.*
*-- UVa coach Bruce Arena on not having a clear-cut champion*

**The power of the one who controls the weather is
beyond anything we can imagine,
but so is his love for us.**

## DAY 97

# THE PRIZE

### Read Philippians 3:10-16.

*"I press on toward the goal to win the prize for which God has called me heavenward in Christ Jesus" (v. 14).*

One national publication named UVa sophomore linebacker Randy Neal its defensive player of the week -- and he was totally embarrassed about it.

The Cavs opened the 1992 season by winning their first five games behind fifth-year quarterback Bobby Goodman and star running back Terry Kirby. A promising season fell apart, though, when Kirby suffered a broken shoulder blade against Clemson. The Cavs were only 6-4 when they headed into Lane Stadium for the season finale against Virginia Tech.

Kirby needed only seventy-six yards to break John Papit's school rushing record, and running backs coach Ken Mack vowed to do everything he could to get Kirby the record. As it turned out, Kirby didn't need any help. Sore shoulder and all, he lugged the ball twenty-six times for 185 yards to lead the Cavaliers to a thrilling 41-38 win.

Tech outgained Virginia by more than two hundred yards and held the ball for more than 35 minutes. The difference, though, was the 21 points the Cavs' defense and special teams either set up or scored. Redshirt freshman Kareem Martin made a big play by blocking a punt that led to a Kirby touchdown.

But Neal was the defensive star of the day, intercepting two passes and returning them both for touchdowns. Those big plays earned him the national recognition, which embarrassed Neal because the Cavs had given up so many yards and points. He also wasn't particularly pleased with his overall play, saying, "I got handled by this guy [Tech center Jim Pyne] the whole game."

Even the most modest and self-effacing among us -- such as Randy Neal -- can't help but be pleased by prizes and honors. They symbolize the approval and appreciation of others, whether it's an All-American team, an Employee of the Month trophy, a plaque for sales achievement, or the sign declaring yours as the neighborhood's prettiest yard.

Such prizes and awards are often the culmination of the pursuit of personal achievement and accomplishment. They represent accolades and recognition from the world. Nothing is inherently wrong with any of that as long as we keep them in perspective.

That is, we must never let awards become such idols that we worship or lower our sight from the greatest prize of all and the only one truly worth winning. It's one that won't rust, collect dust, or leave us wondering why we worked so hard to win it in the first place. The ultimate prize is eternal life, and it's ours through Jesus Christ.

*I wasn't happy after the game because I knew I hadn't really done what I was supposed to do.*
*-- Randy Neal on the 1992 Tech game*

**The greatest prize of all doesn't require competition to claim it; God has it ready to hand to you through Jesus Christ.**

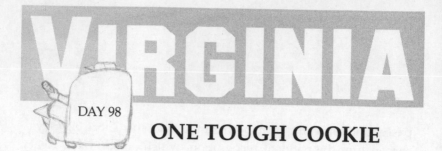

# ONE TOUGH COOKIE

### Read 2 Corinthians 11:21b-29.

*"Besides everything else, I face daily the pressure of my concern for all the churches" (v. 28).*

**V**irginia's first head football coach was so tough that he once chastised his players at practice for their reluctance to pile on him until he couldn't breathe.

Virginia hired John P. "Johnny" Poe as its first football coach in 1893. Poe was a former star at Princeton, and he brought immediate success to the program with an 8-3 record in '93, the school's best ever. His 1894 team was 8-2 and set a school record by scoring 414 points, a mark not broken until George Welsh's prolific 1990 team, more than a hundred years later. After two seasons, Poe left to coach at the U.S. Naval Academy and was killed in France during World War I. Princeton named its football field after him.

The success Virginia enjoyed during Poe's two seasons at the helm could be attributed to the toughness he brought to the program. Football in its early days was an exceptionally brutal game, and that's the way Poe coached it.

For instance, piling on was allowed, even encouraged. At practice one day, Poe instructed his squad on the finer techniques of piling on. He fell on the ball and told his players to pile on him. As team member Murray M. McGuire put it, since Poe was the coach, the players "left him room to breathe," which only incensed the head man. Said McGuire, "He expressed the greatest dissatisfaction and yelled at the top of his voice that no one was on his head." Perhaps tongue in cheek, McGuire wrote that the tough head coach "had no further cause to complain that day or the succeeding day, because of the consideration shown his feelings or his head."

You don't have to be a college football coach to be tough. In America today, toughness isn't restricted to physical accomplishments and brute strength. Going to work every morning even when you feel bad, sticking by your rules for your children in a society that ridicules parental authority, making hard decisions about your aging parents' care often over their objections — you've got to be tough every day just to live honorably, decently, and justly.

Living faithfully requires toughness, too, though in America chances are you won't be imprisoned, stoned, or flogged this week for your faith as Paul was. Still, contemporary society exerts subtle, psychological, daily pressures on you to turn your back on your faith and your values. Popular culture promotes promiscuity, atheism, and gutter language; your children's schools have kicked God out; the corporate culture advocates amorality before the shrine of the almighty dollar.

You have to hang tough to keep the faith.

*Winning isn't imperative, but getting tougher in the fourth quarter is.*
*— Bear Bryant*

**Life demands more than mere physical toughness;**
**you must be spiritually tough too.**

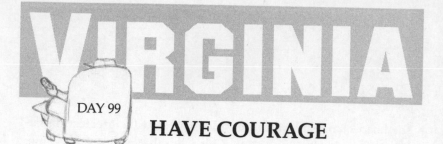

DAY 99

# HAVE COURAGE

### Read 1 Corinthians 16:13-14.

*"Be on your guard; stand firm in the faith; be men of courage; be strong" (v. 13).*

One of the greatest and most unlikely players in Virginia football history risked everything -- twice -- in courageous fashion to achieve his life's goals.

Jim Bakhtiar was 11 years old when he left his native Iran in 1946 to pursue an education in America. As a freshman in high school, he returned to Iran to visit his father. Before he left, he told his father he wanted to become an All-American football player and a doctor, and his father advised him to move out of his mother's house and live on his own. He did, supporting himself as a teenager by managing a gas station at night.

He earned a football scholarship to Virginia, and as the 1955 season began, he was touted as the best sophomore fullback in the country. Because of his unusual background (and his ability), he quickly became a favorite of the fans, who dubbed him the "Persian Prince." Bakhtiar regularly played the whole 60 minutes in games. In the 38-7 slaughter of Virginia Tech in 1957, he scored 26 points, including the place kicking. He set ACC records for rushing yards, attempts, and most 100-yard games. As a senior in 1957, he was first-team All-America.

After he became a doctor, he returned to Iran. When the Islamic revolution broke out, he was arrested one night and imprisoned for a month. He decided on another courageous move, leading his family in June 1982 in a daring escape with nothing but the clothes on their backs. They rode on horseback and hid out in caves in the daytime. When Bakhtiar made it to America, former coaches and teammates helped him resume his medical career.

When we speak of courage, we often think of heroic actions such as that displayed by soldiers during wartime or firefighters during an inferno. But as Jim Bakhtiar's life demonstrates, sometimes courage means moving determinedly ahead with what we know we must do despite severe obstacles.

Certainly Bakhtiar was afraid as he sat in prison. What made his daily life courageous and admirable was not the absence of fear, which usually results from foolhardiness or a dearth of relevant information. Rather, his courage showed itself in his determined refusal to let fear debilitate him.

This is the courage God calls upon us to demonstrate in our faith lives. When Paul urged the Christians in Corinth to "be men of courage," he wasn't telling them to rush into burning buildings. He was admonishing them to be strong and sure in their faith in Jesus Christ. This courageous attitude is an absolute necessity for American Christians today when our faith is under attack as never before. Our courage reveals itself in our proclaiming the name of Jesus, no matter what forces are arrayed against us.

*I feel like I just did what I had to do.*
*-- Jim Bakhtiar on his decision to move out on his own as a teenager*

**To be courageous for Jesus is to speak his name**
**boldly no matter the forces arrayed against us.**

# VIRGINIA

## THE END

### Read Revelation 22:1-17.

*"I am the Alpha and the Omega, the First and the Last, the Beginning and the End" (v. 13).*

One strike and Virginia had a win. One strike and Wake Forest had a win. Finally, on the third try, one of the most dramatic games in UVa baseball history ended.

"This is one that you'll always remember," said UVa head coach Dennis Womack about the meeting between the Cavs and the Demon Deacons on May 23, 2003, in the ACC Tournament. The game was lose and go home, and Wake Forest took control early with a spectacular start; after six batters, the Deacs led 5-0.

But the Cavs picked themselves up and got back in the game with three runs in the bottom of the first. After that, they just kept chipping away. They tied the game in the fifth and went ahead 9-7 with a pair in the seventh.

Then in the top of the ninth, the Cavaliers were one strike away from a 9-7 win that would let them play another day. Two outs. 1-2 count. Bases loaded. As the UVa fans gasped in dismay, the Demon Deacon batter played the devil by blasting a home run.

In the bottom of the ninth, outfielder Paul Gillispie doubled and catcher Scott Headd singled. But a sacrifice and a groundout and two straight strikes on freshman Matt Dunn left the Cavs within one strike of ending the game. "I didn't really feel any pressure," Dunn said after the game. He must not have because he

lashed a single up the middle, tying the game at 11.

Wake Forest put runners at second and third in the top of the tenth, but sophomore Adam Laird got a strikeout. In the bottom of the tenth, the long-delayed end came suddenly. Three-time All-America Joe Koshansky hit a long foul out of the stadium on the first pitch and then followed that up with a line shot home run. The Cavs moved on; Wake's season had ended.

Every baseball game -- even a dramatic one -- is just another example of one of life's basic truths: Everything ends. Even the stars have a life cycle, though admittedly it's rather lengthy. Erosion eventually will wear a boulder to a pebble. Life itself is temporary; all living things have a beginning and an end.

Within the framework of our individual lifetimes, we meet endings. Loved ones, friends, and pets die; relationships fracture; jobs dry up; our health, clothes, lawn mowers, TV sets – they all wear out. Even this world as we know it will end.

But one of the greatest ironies of God's gift of life is that not even death is immune from the great truth of creation that all things must end. That's because through Jesus' life, death, and resurrection, God himself acted to end any power death once had over life. In other words, because of Jesus, the end of life has ended. Eternity is ours for the claiming.

*I was kind of trying to hit a home run. The game was back and forth all day. I wanted to go up there and try and end it.*
*-- Joe Koshansky on his game-ending home run*

**Everything ends; thanks to Jesus Christ,**
**so does death.**

# VIRGINIA

## NOTES
### (by Devotion Day Number)

1    After several years of playing around . . . president of the "Foot Ball Association.": Jerry Ratcliffe, *The University of Virginia Football Vault: The History of the Cavaliers* (Atlanta: Whitman Publishing, LLC, 2008), p. 7.

1    instructed the neophytes on the game's . . . the Potomac River to field a football team.: Ratcliffe, *The University of Virginia Football* Vault, p. 8.

2    Straight pain tolerance.": Kris Wright, "Sherrill Showing Toughness," *TheSabre.com*, Jan. 3, 2011, http://www.thesabre.com/archives/2011/sabremail0477.html, Jan. 20, 2011.

2    "He's the toughest guy on this team . . . when he was not in the gym.: Wright.

2    The bone is healed enough where it's not really going to break more.: Wright.

3    "He could have made excuses . . . ever have to take me out."": Ratcliffe, *Virginia Football Vault*, p. 130.

3    He started some of the younger . . . record-setting running back Wali Lundy.: Ratcliffe, *Virginia Football Vault*, p. 130.

3    [Matt Schaub's] resiliency was certainly the backbone of that team.: Ratcliffe, *Virginia Football Vault*, p. 130.

4    "a great kid and a good player," . . . Just take care of yourself.": Doug Doughty and Roland Lazenby, *'Hoos 'N' Hokies* (Dallas: Taylor Publishing Company, 1995), p. 113.

4    No sooner had the jubilant . . . at a Washington-area McDonald's.: Doughty and Lazenby, p. 113.

4    No one knows when he is . . . come in the blink of an eye.: Jim & Julie S. Bettinger, *The Book of Bowden* (Nashville: TowleHouse Publishing, 2001), p. 21.

5    Virginia went on the attack with 11 seconds left: Rob Daniels, *Arena Ball* (Lenexa, KS: Quality Sports Publications, 1994), p. 52.

5    Lyle Yorks lofted a pass . . . the officials got it right.: Daniels, p. 53.

5    Coach Bruce Arena made a key strategic . . . with a fresh Tom Henske.: Daniels, p. 55.

6    You worried?" "Nah." "Me neither.": Doug Doughty, "One More Week as No. 1?" *The Roanoke Times*, 21 Oct. 1990.

6    "You had to be thinking 'upset,'": Doughty, "One More Week as No. 1?"

6    apparently missing hospitalized All-ACC . . . had been designated for a redshirt.: Doughty, "One More Week as No. 1?"

6    I can't be agitated . . . a pass or don't score.: Doughty, "One More Week as No. 1?"

7    "He's really a significant athlete,": Katrina Waugh, "Hall's Repertoire Is Growing," *The Roanoke Times*, 11 Oct. 2009.

7    What hasn't he done . . . he's always looked athletic.: Waugh, "Hall's Repertoire Is Growing."

8    The opening of University Hall in 1965 brought with it a new sense of optimism: Chris Graham and Patrick Hite, *Mad About U* (Waynesboro, VA: Augusta Free Press, 2006), p. 47.

8    "The facilities were just 10 times better,": Graham and Hite, p. 48.

8    his mother came to a freshman game . . . winning sport at the University.: Graham and Hite, p. 49.

8    "the shot heard round the Hall": Graham and Hite, p. 41.

8    Hobgood said that in short order U . . . dynamic of the program had changed,": Graham and Hite, p. 50.

8    I'm not too proud to change. I like to win too much.: Bettinger, p. 15.

9    declaring he'd bought Welsh a headstone . . . a change in a man's career.: Ratcliffe, *Virginia Football Vault*, p. 89.

9    "If it's a graveyard, it's a pretty nice graveyard,": Ratcliffe, *Virginia Football Vault*, p. 89.

9    "I didn't come here to win four games.": Ratcliffe, *Virginia Football Vault*, p. 90.

9    "unprecedented heights": Ratcliffe, *Virginia Football Vault*, p. 90.

10   "The Cavaliers have once again fallen under the spell.": Doughty and Lazenby, p. 83.

10   "The fans at Virginia are tired of . . . Nothing else will suffice.": Doughty and Lazenby, pp. 85-86.

10   head coach Bill Elias had installed . . . but finding a way out.": Doughty and Lazenby, p. 85.

11   "We did not scout this," . . . didn't give us anything easy,": Katrina Waugh, "Wright, Cavs Pull Plug on Horror Flick," *The Roanoke Times*, Jan. 12, 2009.

11   Coach Debbie Ryan went to . . . and six defensive rebounds.: Waugh, "Wright, Cavs Pull Plug."

12   He saw a bumper sticker that read . . . I saw it about three times.": Doughty and Lazenby, p. 144.

12   "The Virginia Tech police picked . . . walked to the locker room.': Doughty and Lazenby, p. 145.

12   "a purely selfish matter . . . misfortune or frustration": Bruce T. Dahlberg, "Anger," *The Interpreter's Dictionary of the Bible* (Nashville: Abingdon Press, 1962), Vol. 1, p. 136.

12   By the time we got to the stadium, I was furious.: Doughty and Lazenby, p. 145.

13   Virginia head coach Dom Starsia found . . . We wanted this game to be over,".: John Walters, "That

Cavalier Attitude," *Sports Illustrated*, June 7, 1999, http://sportsillustrated.cnn.com/vault/
    article/magazine/MAG1016082/index.htm, Jan. 26, 2011.

13    Early in the quarter, Curtis . . . "I'm seriously stressed,": Walters.

13    She remained in the stands . . . "You can always get another wedding ring.": Walters.

13    She left the stadium with . . . her ring was in there somewhere.: Walters.

13    I'm not having a good jewelry day, but I'm having a great lacrosse day.: Walters.

14    "stubbornly persisted in pretending the other didn't exist.": Doughty and Lazenby, p. 29.

14    "Clearly, the two schools were the best . . . opportunities for classic showdowns.": Doughty and
    Lazenby, pp. 29-30.

14    Part of the reason behind the . . . rendered such attempts futile.: Doughty and Lazenby, p. 30.

14    Over the years, though, the attitudes . . . what had caused the breach.: Doughty and Lazenby, p. 34.

14    saw the importance of reviving the series,: Doughty and Lazenby, p. 34.

14    There was too much feeling between the two teams.: Doughty and Lazenby, p. 29.

15    Virginia head football coach Frank Murray came up . . . coaches snickered openly at the idea.:
    Doughty and Lazenby, p. 52.

15    After the 1940 UVA season . . . he wouldn't touch the ball as often.: Doughty and Lazenby, p. 51.

15    The coach decided to put Dudley in at left halfback . . . too long to teach it to the players.: Doughty
    and Lazenby, p. 52.

16    the ushers dressed in tuxedos . . . rather than a basketball game.: Graham and Hite, p. 78.

16    he "would ride into the sunset a conquering hero.": Graham and Hite, p. 78.

16    as the crowd gasped,: Graham and Hite, p. 79.

16    It was a great way to end . . . end a career at University Hall.: Graham and Hite, p. 80.

17    coaching was not part of his master plan. . . . went into full remission with a transplant.: Doug
    Doughty, "Thankful for All of Life's Opportunities," *The Roanoke Times*, Aug. 29, 2010.

17    I've been blessed with my life . . . with me as a vehicle.: Doughty, "Thankful for All of Life's
    Opportunities."

18    he suffered a broken foot two days . . . in the time since his first surgery.: Doug Doughty, "'He's a
    Walking Miracle,'" *The Roanoke Times*, April 14, 2005.

18    He's a walking miracle in my estimation.: Doughty, "'He's a Walking Miracle.'"

19    "is widely considered the best woman basketball player ever to emerge from the University":
    "Dawn Staley Gives Pep Talk to U.Va. Graduates," *UVatoday*, May 16, 2009, http://www.
    virginia.edu/uvatoday/newsRelease.php?id=8712, Jan. 26, 2011.

19    "Dawn is special to the game. . . . and straightened the red lines.: Douglas S. Looney, "A Blazing
    Dawn," *Sports Illustrated*, Nov. 19, 1990, http://sportsillustrated.cnn.com/vault/article/
    magazine/MAG1106107/index.htm, Jan. 26, 2011.

19    She was the perfect player.: Looney.

20    Virginia pounded Duke for three quarters, and then the real fighting began.": Doug Doughty,
    "Inspired by Brawl, Cavaliers Deck Blue Devils 35-0," *The Roanoke Times*, Sept. 26, 1993.

20    flattened the thief along the sideline . . . when they started looking for numbers.". Doughty,
    "Inspired by Brawl."

20    Somewhere some hockey player . . . 'Look at those football players.': Doughty, "Inspired by Brawl."

21    When he was 10 years old, . . . his first glimpse of UVa football.: Cayce Trexel, "Dr. Risher -- UVa's
    Oldest Football Alumnus -- Turns 100," *VirginiaSports.com*, May 11, 2010, http://www.
    virginiasports.com/View/Article.dbml?DB_OEM_ID=17800, Jan. 19, 2011.

21    Actually getting in to a game . . . I'm still a small peg in the group.": Trexel.

21    I'd always been interested in [football], but after I saw Virginia play, I loved it.: Trexel.

22    Chris grew up in a big house . . . Longs refer to Sintim as their fourth son.: Lee Jenkins, "The
    Education of Chris Long," *Sports Illustrated*, March 10, 2008, http://sportsillustrated.cnn.
    com/vault/article/magazine/MAG1109935/index.html, Jan. 26, 2011.

22    When Chris tried out for his first . . . his son would stick with the game.: Lee Jenkins.

22    I was obviously wrong about Chris.: Lee Jenkins.

23    Our kid is crazy." . . . he had a chance to be special.": Lars Anderson, "World of Talent," *Sports
    Illustrated*, Nov. 4, 2002, http://sportsillustrated.cnn.com/vault/article/magazine/
    MAG1027317/index.html, Jan. 26, 2011.

24    the two football programs were headed . . . that they were dodging the Hokies.: Doughty and
    Lazenby, p. 95.

24    Tech athletic director Frank Moseley . . . bring the Cavs to Lane Stadium in 1970.: Doughty and
    Lazenby, p. 97.

24    the Hokies established as prohibitive favorites.: Doughty and Lazenby, p. 99.

24    "We never did hear that $40,000 scoreboard of theirs,": Doughty and Lazenby,
    p. 99.

25    he received some coaching advice: Speed it up a bit, son.: Doug Doughty, "Kick Wobbles, But Ties," *The Roanoke Times*, Oct. 19, 2008.

25    "It was a real tense moment,": Doughty, "Kick Wobbles, But Ties."

26    "Nobody really gave us a shot to win the game,": Graham and Hite, p. 128.

26    "Richard was, I mean, he was white-hot that night,": Graham and Hite, p. 128.

26    he ran to save the ball from going . . . and hit the shot.: Graham and Hite, p. 127.

26    "It was that kind of night,": Graham and Hite, p. 127.

26    he'd look over to Carolina head coach . . . enjoyed it as much as anyone else.": Graham and Hite, p. 129.

27    one writer called it "unthinkable.": Doug Doughty, "Cavaliers Freshman Evans Catches on Fast," *The Roanoke Times*, Sept. 27, 1999.

27    the head coach of 27 years couldn't . . . done it before [but] not much,": Doug Doughty, "Welsh Makes Bold Call," *The Roanoke Times*, Sept. 28, 1999.

27    Welsh hinted that he . . . decided on a quarterback sneak.: Doughty, "Welsh Makes Bold Call."

27    Does Coach Welsh know about it?: Doughty, "Cavaliers Freshman Evans Catches on Fast."

28    "the region of death." . . . themselves busy the entire day,": Doug Doughty, "Cavaliers Love the Night Life," *The Roanoke Times*, June 2, 2009.

28    Arico throwing the final pitch at 2:19 a.m. EDT: Doughty, "Cavaliers Love the Night Life."

29    As one writer put it, Virginia's defense was in the backfield so quickly "they seemed to know the play.": Doughty and Lazenby, p. 158.

29    Toliver admitted that one of the Tech linemen . . . something bad went wrong.": Doughty and Lazenby, p. 158.

29    "The guard had been leaning," . . . sometimes the defense got badly burned.: Doughty and Lazenby, p. 161.

29    I remember watching the play on film and just shaking my head.: Doughty and Lazenby, p. 158.

30    In the first eight meetings, UVa "mercilessly pounded" the Hokies,: Doughty and Lazenby, p. 21.

30    who was playing his seventh season of college football: Doughty and Lazenby, p. 21.

30    Virginia players groused that Tech . . . rejected this notion outright.: Doughty and Lazenby, p. 22.

30    Two days before the game, UVa . . . decided to come to Charlottesville anyway.: Doughty and Lazenby, p. 24.

30    The publicity brought out the largest crowd . . . was read aloud to the crowd,: Doughty and Lazenby, p. 25.

31    He knew then that he wanted . . . considered coaching women before,: Graham and Hite, p. 93.

31    "I think the reason . . . I knew what I was doing,": Graham and Hite, pp. 93-94.

31    Corrigan had plans to make . . . to pay $1,600 a year for tuition,: Graham and Hite, p. 94.

32    a defense that was ranked in the top 25 nationally in seven different categories.: Doug Doughty, "Cavs Cruise to Their 4th Straight Victory," *The Roanoke Times*, Sept. 30, 2007.

32    "I probably had about 50 people . . . them to give us another chance.": Doughty, "Cavs Cruise."

33    The Spartan player jockeying at the line . . . "superhero Elastic Man or Stretch Armstrong.": Jerry Ratcliffe, "Sene Makes His Rare Baskets Count," *Cavalier Insider*, Dec. 20, 2010, http://www2.cavalierinsider.com/sports/2010/dec/20, Feb. 5, 2011.

34    Guepe's players considered him a stern . . . to be honest with you,": Doughty and Lazenby, p. 58.

34    Guepe did his service during World War II . . . stupid defenses would go out with us,": Doughty and Lazenby, p. 59.

34    "he didn't care if his recruits could . . . "They wouldn't look at him.": Doughty and Lazenby, p. 59.

35    "I said we could win but nobody believed me,": Larry Keith, "Virginia Crashes the Party," *Sports Illustrated*, March 15, 1976, http://sportsillustrated.cnn.com/vault/article/magazine/MAG1090846/index.htm, Jan. 26, 2011.

35    Before the tournament, some made motel . . . weaknesses that can be attacked,": Keith.

35    The Cavs used an aggressive man-to-man defense and a deliberate offense to stay close.: Keith.

35    "despicable, vile, unprincipled scoundrels.": John MacArthur, *Twelve Ordinary Men* (Nashville: W Publishing Group, 2002), p. 152.

35    I don't consider this an upset.: Keith.

36    Out of high school, Moore narrowed . . . before his football eligibility had expired.: Doughty and Lazenby, p. 174.

36    We're going to live to regret this.: Doughty and Lazenby, p. 174.

37    The Cavaliers stunned a crowd of 45,100 . . . college football's traditional powers.": Doug Doughty, "Barber, 'Hoos Hook 'Horns," *The Roanoke Times*, Sept. 29, 1996.

37    "There's not that much difference . . . had nothing go their way.": Doughty, "Barber, 'Hoos Hook 'Horns."

37    scoring on three consecutive runs: Doughty, "Barber, 'Hoos Hook 'Horns."

37 "You get to a point where . . . 'They can't stop us,'": Doughty, "Barber, 'Hoos Hook 'Horns.'"

38 Alexander committed back-to-back . . . We'd taken him out once already.": Doug Doughty, "Alexander Saves Best for Last," *The Roanoke Times*, Jan. 15, 1995.

38 "may be remembered as the greatest comeback in school history.": Doug Doughty, "A Devil of a Rally for Cavs," *The Roanoke Times*, Jan. 15, 1995.

38 "I don't know what got into him,": Doughty, "Alexander Saves Best for Last."

38 "I'm definitely dumbfounded," . . . believe it was happening.": Doughty, "A Devil of a Rally."

38 After his turnovers, . . . make the best of the situation,": Doughty, "Alexander Saves Best for Last."

38 We decided to stay with him a little bit longer. It's fortunate we did.: Doughty, "Alexander Saves Best for Last."

39 a move he always regretted.: Ratcliffe, *Virginia Football Vault*, p. 85.

39 Concerned because Lawrence was part . . . a three-year deal.: Ratcliffe, *Virginia Football Vault*, p. 85.

39 He went to Corrigan after . . . assistants were taken care of.: Ratcliffe, *Virginia Football Vault*, p. 85.

40 The coaches caught it just before . . . when 12 went undetected.": Doug Doughty, "Cavs Have Officials to Thank for TD," *The Roanoke Times*, Nov. 22, 2006.

41 the Cavs and Virginia Tech were tied . . . which still showed 24 seconds.: Graham and Hite, p. 107.

41 the ref said she used her own internal . . . of calling for a jump ball.: Graham and Hite, p. 108.

41 With a much taller center, . . . the length of the floor to score,: Graham and Hite, p. 108.

41 "The poor girl takes the ball . . . and calls her for traveling.": Graham and Hite, pp. 108-09.

41 Bonner didn't care whether it was a . . . Instead, Stenzel shot and scored.: Graham and Hite, p. 109.

42 "the turning point in the Cavaliers' football program": Doughty and Lazenby, p. 146.

42 "We've got to beat these guys one . . . his assistant coaches before the 1984 Tech came.: Doughty and Lazenby, p. 147.

42 Majkowski later said he thought . . . looked like the Rubber Man,": Doughty and Lazenby, p. 146.

42 I shall never forget . . . just an unbelievable catch.: Doughty and Lazenby, p. 146.

43 I was like, 'I did that.'": Doug Doughty, "Rogers Saves Best for Last.": *The Roanoke Times*, March 11, 2003.

43 Less than two minutes into the . . . "I was like, 'I did that.": Doughty, "Rogers Saves Best for Last."

43 "I couldn't believe it," . . . "I was stunned.": Doughty, "Rogers Saves Best for Last."

43 That's the best he's played in four years.: Doughty, "Rogers Saves Best for Last."

44 Virginia managed to win by her usual slugging.": Doughty and Lazenby, p. 20.

44 "was an embarrassment for the Hokies.": Doughty and Lazenby, p. 18.

44 "at times showed an unnecessary . . . unable to hold the score down.": Doughty and Lazenby, p. 18.

44 After the game, the Hokie manager . . . run over the Hokies 395 yards to 145.: Doughty and Lazenby, p. 18.

44 "We were sorry to learn that VPI . . . badly treated in the game.": Doughty and Lazenby, pp. 18, 20.

44 The writer apologized for UVa's . . . "so down on your luck here": Doughty and Lazenby, p. 20.

44 which even the Cavalier newspaper admitted . . . should have been blown dead.: Doughty and Lazenby, pp. 20-21.

44 The VPI team gave an exhibition of puerile behavior at every decision of the umpire.: Doughty and Lazenby, p. 20.

45 Honaker didn't have a stoplight -- and definitely not a stoplight.": Doug Doughty, "Good Catch for Cavaliers," *The Roanoke Times*, Sept. 4, 2002.

46 "I was having a tough time," . . . I didn't belong at this level,": Doug Doughty, "One Slip of Paper Provided All the Inspiration," *The Roanoke Times*, Jan. 29, 1990.

46 "I was really pumped up for . . . assigned to guard Coles all night.: Doughty, "One Slip of Paper."

46 When he says something like that, it sticks with you.: Doughty, "One Slip of Paper."

47 Because of the defense, McMullen decided . . . and shouted out, "Same play, same play.": Doug Doughty, "Groh's Cavs Full of Surprises," *The Roanoke Times*, Nov. 11, 2001.

47 three confident Tech receivers converged on the receiver, leaving Pearlman open.: Doug Doughty, "Cavaliers Hook Yellow Jackets in Scott," *The Roanoke Times*, Nov. 11, 2001.

47 Desperate times call for desperate measures.: Doughty, "Cavaliers Hook Yellow Jackets in Scott."

48 on a field that was cut out of a mountainside . . . touchdown easily from there.": Doughty and Lazenby, p. 48.

48 Now what are you going to say to Dudley?: Doughty and Lazenby, p. 48.

49 One September evening in 1991, . . . "We didn't expect it to come true.": Kelly Whiteside, "Four-peat," *Sports Illustrated*, Dec. 19, 1994, http://sportsillustrated.cnn.com/vault/article/magazine/MAG1006092/index.htm, Jan. 26, 2011.

49 "We're like regulars here," . . . the team should rent a condo.: Whiteside.

50 "a period of losing and mediocrity": Doughty and Lazenby, p. 64.

50 "It appeared to me that the administration . . . excited about a successful athletic program.": Doughty and Lazenby, pp. 63-64.

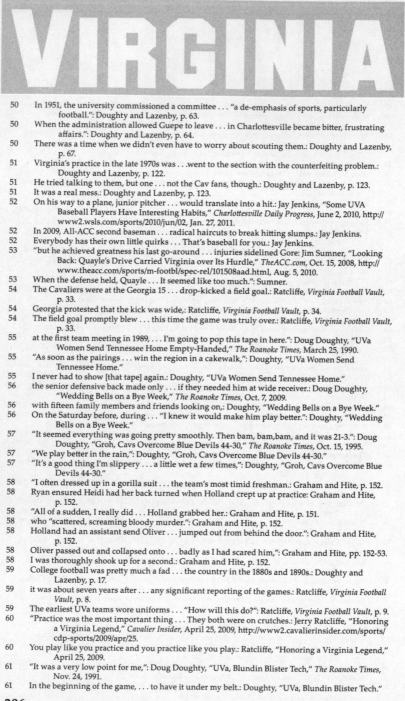

# VIRGINIA

50　In 1951, the university commissioned a committee . . . "a de-emphasis of sports, particularly football.": Doughty and Lazenby, p. 63.

50　When the administration allowed Guepe to leave . . . in Charlottesville became bitter, frustrating affairs.": Doughty and Lazenby, p. 64.

50　There was a time when we didn't even have to worry about scouting them.: Doughty and Lazenby, p. 67.

51　Virginia's practice in the late 1970s was . . .went to the section with the counterfeiting problem.: Doughty and Lazenby, p. 122.

51　He tried talking to them, but one . . . not the Cav fans, though.: Doughty and Lazenby, p. 123.

51　It was a real mess.: Doughty and Lazenby, p. 123.

52　On his way to a plane, junior pitcher . . . would translate into a hit.: Jay Jenkins, "Some UVA Baseball Players Have Interesting Habits," *Charlottesville Daily Progress*, June 2, 2010, http://www2.wsls.com/sports/2010/jun/02, Jan. 27, 2011.

52　In 2009, All-ACC second baseman . . . radical haircuts to break hitting slumps.: Jay Jenkins.

52　Everybody has their own little quirks . . . That's baseball for you.: Jay Jenkins.

53　"but he achieved greatness his last go-around . . . injuries sidelined Gore: Jim Sumner, "Looking Back: Quayle's Drive Carried Virginia over Its Hurdle," *TheACC.com*, Oct. 15, 2008, http://www.theacc.com/sports/m-footbl/spec-rel/101508aad.html, Aug. 5, 2010.

53　When the defense held, Quayle . . . It seemed like too much.": Sumner.

54　The Cavaliers were at the Georgia 15 . . . drop-kicked a field goal.: Ratcliffe, *Virginia Football Vault*, p. 33.

54　Georgia protested that the kick was wide,: Ratcliffe, *Virginia Football Vault*, p. 34.

54　The field goal promptly blew . . . this time the game was truly over.: Ratcliffe, *Virginia Football Vault*, p. 33.

55　at the first team meeting in 1989, . . . I'm going to pop this tape in here.": Doug Doughty, "UVa Women Send Tennessee Home Empty-Handed," *The Roanoke Times*, March 25, 1990.

55　"As soon as the pairings . . . win the region in a cakewalk,": Doughty, "UVa Women Send Tennessee Home."

55　I never had to show [that tape] again.: Doughty, "UVa Women Send Tennessee Home."

56　the senior defensive back made only . . . if they needed him at wide receiver.: Doug Doughty, "Wedding Bells on a Bye Week," *The Roanoke Times*, Oct. 7, 2009.

56　with fifteen family members and friends looking on,: Doughty, "Wedding Bells on a Bye Week."

56　On the Saturday before, during . . . "I knew it would make him play better.": Doughty, "Wedding Bells on a Bye Week."

57　"It seemed everything was going pretty smoothly. Then bam, bam,bam, and it was 21-3.": Doug Doughty, "Groh, Cavs Overcome Blue Devils 44-30," *The Roanoke Times*, Oct. 15, 1995.

57　"We play better in the rain,": Doughty, "Groh, Cavs Overcome Blue Devils 44-30."

57　"It's a good thing I'm slippery . . . a little wet a few times,": Doughty, "Groh, Cavs Overcome Blue Devils 44-30."

58　"I often dressed up in a gorilla suit . . . the team's most timid freshman.: Graham and Hite, p. 152.

58　Ryan ensured Heidi had her back turned when Holland crept up at practice: Graham and Hite, p. 152.

58　"All of a sudden, I really did . . . Holland grabbed her.: Graham and Hite, p. 151.

58　who "scattered, screaming bloody murder.": Graham and Hite, p. 152.

58　Holland had an assistant send Oliver . . . jumped out from behind the door.": Graham and Hite, p. 152.

58　Oliver passed out and collapsed onto . . . badly as I had scared him,": Graham and Hite, pp. 152-53.

58　I was thoroughly shook up for a second.: Graham and Hite, p. 152.

59　College football was pretty much a fad . . . the country in the 1880s and 1890s.: Doughty and Lazenby, p. 17.

59　it was about seven years after . . . any significant reporting of the games.: Ratcliffe, *Virginia Football Vault*, p. 8.

59　The earliest UVa teams wore uniforms . . . "How will this do?": Ratcliffe, *Virginia Football Vault*, p. 9.

60　"Practice was the most important thing . . . They both were on crutches.: Jerry Ratcliffe, "Honoring a Virginia Legend," *Cavalier Insider*, April 25, 2009, http://www2.cavalierinsider.com/sports/cdp-sports/2009/apr/25.

60　You play like you practice and you practice like you play.: Ratcliffe, "Honoring a Virginia Legend," April 25, 2009.

61　"It was a very low point for me,": Doug Doughty, "UVa, Blundin Blister Tech," *The Roanoke Times*, Nov. 24, 1991.

61　In the beginning of the game, . . . to have it under my belt.: Doughty, "UVa, Blundin Blister Tech."

**206**

62    Jones vented his frustration by . . . Arizona that I was healed up,": Jerry Ratcliffe, "Honoring a Virginia Institution," *Cavalier Insider*, June 8, 2008, http://www2.cavalierinsider.com/sports/cdp-sports/2008/jun/08.

62    Sometimes you have to play with a little pain.: Justin A. Rice "Spiller Delivers Knockout Blow." *The State*, Nov. 2, 2008, http://docs.newsbank.com/s/InfoWeb/aggdocs/NewsBank/12434A3FE4C4F2D8, May 6, 2009.

63    He landed the job through a . . . around the corner from Memorial Gym.: Doug Doughty, "UVa Gave Shula a Start 50 Years Ago," *The Roanoke Times*, Feb. 19, 2008.

63    "Now, Sonny, he was my guy," . . . he'll be a short-timer here.": Doughty, "UVa Gave Shula a Start 50 Years Ago."

63    It was my first coaching job. How could I forget?: Doughty, "UVa Gave Shula a Start 50 Years Ago."

64    During his second semester, he developed . . . no way to play football that day.": Doug Doughty, "A Pain Far Worse Than Losing," *The Roanoke Times*, Sept. 6, 2003.

64    I don't think we were going to win anyway.: Doughty, "A Pain Far Worse Than Losing."

65    "I played on one of the historically bad . . . until Sandell's death in January 2011.: Jerry Ratcliffe, "A Tribute to Bob Sandell," *Cavalier Insider*, Feb. 1, 2011, http://www.mydailyprogress.com/index.php/crunchtime/article.

65    What do you want? . . . Whatever you want, you can have.: Ratcliffe, "A Tribute to Bob Sandell."

66    The first-ever UVa mascot was a black-and-white . . . known as Caninus Magaphonus Pennsylvanus.: "Traditions: Bets and Seal," VirginiaSports.com, http://www.virginiasports.com/ViewArticle.dbml?DB_OEM_ID=1780, Sept. 8, 2010.

66    Local restaurants with signs reading, . . . below, in parentheses, "except Seal.": "Traditions: Beta and Seal."

67    She's absolutely been amazing in . . . to her family and to her teammates.": Jeff White, "Another Crippen Leaves Legacy at UVa," *VirginiaSports.com*, Jan. 25, 1011, http://www.virginiasports.com/ViewArticle.dbml?&ATCLID=205082866&DB_OEM_ID=17800, Jan. 26, 2011.

67    "She never stops smiling, she never stops laughing,": White.

67    "You'll never find a more positive, . . . can't take the joy out of her heart.": White.

67    Claire was wary of following . . . . every time she steps on the block for a race.: White.

67    She just finds the good in everything that you can find good in. She searches for good.: White.

69    He failed the ninth grade: "Branden Albert," *Wikipedia, the free encyclopedia*, http://en.wikipedia.org/wiki/Branden_Albert, Feb. 2, 2011.

69    "I was a very lazy kid when it came to schoolwork,": Doug Doughty, "Follow the Rules and Play Ball," *The Roanoke Times*, Sept. 29, 2005.

69    Albert was in the process of failing . . . to live with his brother,": "Branden Albert."

69    "My brother was very tough on me," . . . he became a football jock.": Doughty, "Follow the Rules and Play Ball."

69    The first couple of months, . . . till I finished my homework.: Doughty, "Follow the Rules and Play Ball."

70    After the 1935 scoreless tie, the UVa . . . Well, they're all the same here at Virginia.": Doughty and Lazenby, p. 44.

70    "Never, since its dedication in 1926, . . . succeeded in defeating the Gobblers on their home field.": Doughty and Lazenby, p. 48.

70    "shattered an 11-year session of Polytechnic domination.": Doughty and Lazenby, p. 49.

71    "Just looking around here right now, . . . would be showering in there.: Doug Doughty, "Cavs Enjoy Posh Surroundings," *The Roanoke Times*, Nov. 9, 2006.

71    He's big time with that shower.: Doughty, "Cavs Enjoy Posh Surroundings."

72    when Rivers finally reached the . . . and he was quite happy about them: Doug Doughty, "From Obscurity to Center Stage," *The Roanoke Times*, Nov. 10, 1999.

72    "How do you explain athletes when they're 21 years old?": Doughty, "From Obscurity to Center Stage."

72    "He threw to the right people . . . to be overcome by emotion.": Doughty: "From Obscurity to Center Stage."

72    He broke down and he deserved his moment of happiness, certainly.: Doughty, "From Obscurity to Center Stage."

73    attendance at the women's games hovered . . . everyone who showed up.: Graham and Hite, p. 114.

73    landed a whole bunch of free publicity . . . what came to be called Hot Dog Night.: Graham and Hite, p. 114.

73    Eight hours before tipoff, fans were in line. . . . more than $10 million in lost revenue.: Graham and Hite, p. 122.

73    People were just everywhere. . . . in the hallways. Just nuts.: Graham and Hite, p. 123.

74    "I didn't think it would be like this.": Doughty and Lazenby, p. 61.

74    Guepe had so much talent on hand that he went to a two-platoon system in '49.: Doughty and Lazenby, p. 62.

74    "They were pitiful," . . . "We didn't have much trouble with the Gobblers.": Doughty and Lazenby, p. 62.

74    the head coach adopted the strange . . . "to see who really wanted to play.": Doughty and Lazenby, p. 62.

74    "hadn't used up all their energy . . . a solid Cavalier forward wall.": Doughty and Lazenby, p. 62.

75    "For years, I was pointed out.": Ratcliffe, *Virginia Football Vault*, p. 32.

75    Until that day, no team from . . . outside of Princeton, Penn, and Harvard.: Ratcliffe, *Virginia Football Vault*, p. 32.

75    Cavalier lineman Claude Moore said beating . . . on the team that beat Yale.": Ratcliffe, *Virginia Football Vault*, p. 32.

76    Forward Jason Clark was slowed . . . worst I've ever felt and played,": Doug Doughty, "Reynolds Shows His Ill Will," *The Roanoke Times*, Jan. 7, 2005.

76    Ninety-eight out of 100 guys . . . 'I've got an upset stomach.': Doughty, "Reynolds Shows His Ill Will."

77    I can give you eight million reasons why North Carolina will beat Virginia,": Doug Doughty, "UVa Rises from Ashes, Singes UNC," *The Roanoke Times*, Nov. 17, 1996.

77    "Today, we were down and just about out,": Doughty, "UVa Rises from Ashes."

78    This night was all about pressure. . . . pressure on a program.": Aaron McFarling, "Pressure-Filled -- Yes, But What a Great Reward," *The Roanoke Times*, Oct. 16, 2005.

78    the Seminole front four went after . . . looked like there were none.": McFarling, "Pressure-Filled."

78    a bank of stadium lights wigged out . . . in the start of the last half.: Doug Doughty, "Time Stands Still," *The Roanoke Times*, Oct. 16, 2005.

79    "arguably the greatest clutch . . . Cavalier uniform since Jeff Lamp.": "Men's Basketball: Cavalier Legends," *virginiasports.com*. http://www.virginiasports.com/ViewArticle.dbml?DB_OEM_ ID=17800&ATCLID=204978167.

79    "made some of his previous heroics seem unimpressive in comparison.: Doug Doughty, "Stith Rescues Cavaliers," *The Roanoke Times*, Jan. 27, 1991.

79    I wanted to be the one to take charge.": Doughty, "Stith Rescues Cavaliers."

79    Over the last 3:14 of . . . but this was unbelievable.": Doughty, "Stith Rescues Cavaliers."

80    On Nov. 13, 1909, in a game against . . . and made it a better game.": Jerry Ratcliffe, "Christian's Death Helped Change Game," *The Daily Progress*, Nov. 14, 2009, http://www.2.dailyprogress. com/sports/cdp-sports-cavinsider/2009/nov/14/christians_death, Oct. 5, 2010.

81    he was on his back when a deflected ball landed in his lap.: Doughty and Lazenby, p. 186.

81    a one-time Spanish exchange student. . . . seeing him play for the first time,: Doughty and Lazenby, p. 185.

81    I saw our players do things that I never have seen in practice.: Doughty and Lazenby, p. 186.

82    Her first task was to find . . . a $27,000 budget and volunteer coaches.: Graham and Hite, p. 97.

82    couldn't find a basketball coach, so she landed the job by default.: Graham and Hite, pp. 97-98.

82    She had no staff, and no secretary . . . planned transportation, arranged schedules,: Graham and Hite, p. 98.

82    washed the one uniform each player had.: Graham and Hite, p. 100.

82    To give the program exposure . . . extremely dangerous to his health.: Graham and Hite, p. 98.

82    The women had to practice . . . they'd drive the females away.: Graham and Hite, p. 101.

82    The men's coach once locked up . . . for the women's game that night.: Graham and Hite, pp. 100-01.

82    Told University Hall had no office . . . storage room and converted it.: Graham and Hite, pp. 101-02.

82    Nobody had any respect for her at all. . . . and keep working away at it.: Graham and Hite, p. 97.

83    It didn't look like . . . and win the ballgame.": Doug Doughty, "Not Road Tripped," *The Roanoke Times*, Jan. 29, 2007.

83    Adrian Joseph scored eight . . . seen a game like this before,': Doughty, "Not Road Tripped."

84    rarely a week goes by . . . and ask him about "the Florida State play.": Jerry Ratcliffe, "Honoring a Virginia Legend," *Cavalier Insider*, Oct. 10, 2009, http://www2.cavalierinsider.com/sports/ cdp-sports/2009/oct/10, Feb. 5, 2011.

84    "perhaps the biggest single defensive play in school history": "Anthony Poindexter Biography," *virginiasports.com*, http://www.virginiasports.com/ViewArticle.dmbl?DB_OEM_ID= 17800&ATCLID=1133515, Feb. 5, 2011.

84    The Noles snapped the ball . . . safety Adrian Burnim stopped Dunn.: Ratcliffe, "Honoring a Virginia Legend," Oct. 10, 2009.

84    I know he didn't. . . . the air like I did.: Ratcliffe, "Honoring a Virginia Legend," Oct. 10, 2009.

85  "frankly, we just took them too lightly.": Wilt Browning, "2007 ACC Football Legend: Virginia's Joe Palumbo," *TheACC.com*, Oct. 16, 2007, http://www.theacc.com/sports/m-footbl/spec-rel/101607/aac.html, Jan. 25, 2011.

85  "Gentlemen," he said. "I want to congratulate . . . want us to come to Dalls.": Browning.

85  there was no outburst, . . . we weren't going anywhere,": Browning.

85  Within hours, the university's president . . . don't want to go professional,": Browning.

85  We felt pretty honored, but we didn't . . . Except to forget it.: Browning.

86  Life is an adventure. I wouldn't want to know what's going to happen next.; Bettinger, p. 74.

87  The report recommended that . . . that football be dropped.: Ratcliffe, *Virginia Football Vault*, p. 64.

87  a study released later in the decade . . . UVa typically had only about 35.: Ratcliffe, *Virginia Football Vault*, p. 79.

87  "They say it can't be done . . . I think I'll try it.": Ratcliffe, *Virginia Football Vault*, p. 80.

87  "In the dressing room before we went . . . of them burst into laughter.: Ratcliffe, *Virginia Football Vault*, pp. 80-81.

87  the fans tore down the goal posts, . . . its National Coach of the Week.: Ratcliffe, *Virginia Football Vault*, p. 80.

88  Cavalier head coach George Welsh . . . "We couldn't lose, could we?": Daniel Uthman, "Pass Play Lucky for UVa," *The Roanoke Times*, Sept. 24, 1995.

88  "yelling a jumble of letters" . . . He hit Jeffers almost in stride: Uthman.

88  There was a miscommunication in the huddle.: Uthman.

89  "probably worked harder than anyone . . . when Evans showed up.": Graham and Hite, p. 159.

89  "I don't know anybody who deserves . . . which she called "sacred.": Graham and Hite, p. 160.

89  I have a lot of good memories . . . and the gym being empty.: Graham and Hite, p. 159.

90  he sought to reverse a series of losses . . . for their ability to withstand hard knocks.": Doughty and Lazenby, p. 45.

90  "a skinny little back with average speed, a mediocre arm, and an awkward kicking style.": Doughty and Lazenby, p. 47.

90  When Dudley came to the bench late in the game, the UNC crowd gave him a standing ovation.: Doughty and Lazenby, p. 53.

90  The Tar Heel players likewise showed . . . carry him off the field to the locker room.: Doughty and Lazenby, p. 47.

91  were 119th among the 119 major teams . . . Journey's "Don't Stop Believing": Doug Doughty, "UVa Reverses Fortune, Trounces Terrapins," *The Roanoke Times*, Oct. 5, 2008.

91  Honestly, I don't think there were . . . we were going to win this game.: Doughty, "UVa Reverses Fortune."

92  Standing 6-foot-4 on the mound, . . . it's something you have to learn.": Bill Hass, "Bill Hass on the ACC: Virginia Faces One More Challenge on Its Long Road to the College World Series," *TheACC.com*, June 12, 2009, http://www.theacc.com/sports/m-basebl/spec-rel/061209aaa.html, Aug. 5, 2010.

92  It's important to flush . . . go after the next hitter.: Bill Hass, "Virginia Faces One More Challenge."

93  The Tigers' head coach, Terry Bowden, was . . . to do with "Something to Prove.": Doug Doughty, "Cavs Repeat the Mantra," *The Roanoke Times*, Sept. 5, 1998.

93  "We got to hush our critics tonight,": Doug Doughty, "Cavs Sorm Past Tigers," *The Roanoke Times*, Sept 4, 1998.

93  I don't want to be stealing . . . had something to prove, too.: Doughty, "Cavs Repeat the Mantra."

94  "If State hadn't been playing, . . . in the Southern Conference Tournament.: Doug Doughty, "Ahead of His Time," *The Roanoke Times*, March 13, 2003.

94  You better stop shooting or you're going to ruin your reputation.: Doughty, "Ahead of His Time."

95  40 of the 47 players on the 1946 football team were vets: Ratcliffe, *Virginia Football Vault*, p. 59.

95  before almost 51,000 spectators: Ratcliffe, *Virginia Football Vault*, p. 61.

95  The Philadelphia Hotel Association claimed . . . for folks from Virginia.: Ratcliffe, *Virginia Football Vault*, p. 62.

95  7,000 horn-tooting, celebrating fans . . . been part of a Penn goal post.: Ratcliffe, *Virginia Football Vault*, p. 63.

96  clear and cold with subzero wind chills and a few flakes of snow.: Daniels, p. 27.

96  Where the field wasn't covered with ice, . . . get up enough energy to scream.": Daniels, p. 29.

96  the two teams "could have played forever . . . and nobody would have scored.": Daniels, p. 30.

96  Some players couldn't feel their feet on the ball, making dribbling upfield virtually impossible.: Daniels, pp. 30-31.

96  The cold affected the ball, . . . "Overtime was cruel and unusual punishment,": Daniels, p. 31.

96  a "theater of the absurd,": Daniels, p. 32.

| 96 | The conditions were such that it wasn't fair for the players to be out there anymore.: Daniels, p. 31. |
| 97 | behind fifth-year quarterback Bobby . . . a broken shoulder blade against Clemson.: Doughty and Lazenby, p. 179. |
| 97 | Kirby needed only seventy-six yards . . . to get Kirby the record.: Doughty and Lazenby, p. 180. |
| 97 | which embarrassed Neal because the . . .[Tech center Jim Pyne] the whole game.": Doughty and Lazenby, p. 181. |
| 97 | I wasn't happy after the game . . . what I was supposed to do.: Doughty and Lazenby, p. 181. |
| 98 | Poe left to coach at the U.S. Naval Academy. . . . each year to a Princeton football player.: Ratcliffe, *Virginia Football Vault*, p. 12. |
| 98 | The success Virginia enjoyed during . . . "left him room to breathe,": Ratcliffe, *Virginia Football Vault*, p. 11. |
| 98 | "He expressed his greatest dissatisfaction . . . shown his feelings or his head.": Ratcliffe, *Virginia Football Vault*, p. 12. |
| 99 | Jim Bakhtiar was 11 years old when he left . . . by managing a gas station at night.: "2009 ACC Football Legends: Jim Bakhtiar, Virginia," *TheACC.com*, Nov. 24, 2009, http://www.theacc.com/sports/m-footbl/spec-rel/112409aac.html, Nov. 1, 2010. |
| 99 | he was touted as the best sophomore . . . who dubbed him the "Persian Prince.": Doughty and Lazenby, p. 76. |
| 99 | After he became a doctor, . . . helped him resume his medical career.: "2009 ACC Football Legends: Jim Bakhtiar, Virginia." |
| 99 | I feel like I just did what I had to do.: "2009 ACC Football Legends: Jim Bakhtiar, Virginia." |
| 100 | "This is one that you'll always remember,": Doug Doughty, "Koshansky's Blast Gives UVa Wild Win," *The Roanoke Times*, May 24, 2003. |
| 100 | As the UVa fans gasped in dismay,: Doughty, "Koshansky's Blast Gives UVa Wild Win." |
| 100 | "I didn't really feel any pressure,": Doughty, "Koshansky's Blast Gives UVa Wild Win." |
| 100 | Joe Koshansky hit a long foul out of the stadium on the first pitch: Doughty, "Koshansky's Blast Gives UVa Wild Win." |
| 100 | I was kind of trying to hit . . . and try and end it.: Doughty, "Koshansky's Blast Gives UVa Wild Win." |

# BIBLIOGRAPHY

"2009 ACC Football Legends: Jim Bakhtiar, Virginia." *TheACC.com*. 24 Nov. 2009. http://www.theacc.com/sports/m-footbl/spec-rel/112409aac.html.

Anderson, Lars. "World of Talent." *Sports Illustrated*. 4 Nov. 2002. http://sportsillustrated.cnn.com/vault/article/magazine/MAG1027317/index.html.

"Anthony Poindexter Biography." *virginiasports.com*. http://www.virginiasports.com/ViewArticle.dbml?DB_OEM_ID=17800&ATCLID=1133515.

Bettinger, Jim & Julie S. *The Book of Bowden*. Nashville: TowleHouse Publishing, 2001.

"Branden Albert." *Wikipedia, the free encyclopedia*. http://en.wikipedia.org/wiki/Branden_Albert.

Browning, Wilt. "2007 ACC Football Legend: Virginia's Joe Palumbo." *TheACC.com*. 16 Oct. 2007. http://www.theacc.com/sports/m-footbl/spec-rel/101607aac.html.

Dahlberg, Bruce T. "Anger." *The Interpreter's Dictionary of the Bible*. Nashville: Abingdon Press, 1962, Vol. 1. 135-37.

Daniels, Rob. *Arena Ball: The Building of Virginia's Soccer Dynasty*.: Lenexa, KS: Quality Sports Publications, 1994.

"Dawn Staley Gives Pep Talk to U.Va. Graduates." *UVatoday*. 16 May 2009. http://www.virginia.edu/uvatoday/newsRelease.php?id=8712.

Doughty, Doug. "A Devil of a Rally for Cavs; UVa Wins at Duke in 2 OTs After Trailing by 23." *The Roanoke Times*. 15 Jan. 1995.

---. "A Pain Far Worse Than Losing: 'I Remember Every Second of Every Minute,' Says

George Welsh." *The Roanoke Times*. 6 Sept. 2003.

---. "Ahead of His Time: 1st ACC Tournament Marked by Wilkinson's 42 Points." *The Roanoke Times*. 13 March 2003.

---. "Alexander Saves Best for Last to Lead Virginia's Stirring Rally." *The Roanoke Times*. 15 Jan. 1995.

---. "Barber, 'Hoos Hook 'Horns: First-Quarter Stampede Sets Up 37-13 Win." *The Roanoke Times*. 29 Sept. 1996.

---. "Cavaliers Freshman Evans Catches on Fast." *The Roanoke Times*. 27 Sept. 1999.

---. "Cavaliers Hook Yellow Jackets in Scott -- Game 10 -- Virginia 39, No. 20 Georgia Tech 38." *The Roanoke Times*, Nov. 11, 2001.

---. "Cavaliers Love the Night Life." *The Roanoke Times*. 2 June 2009.

---. "Cavs Cruise to Their 4th Straight Victory." *The Roanoke Times*. 30 Sept. 2007.

---. "Cavs Enjoy Posh Surroundings." *The Roanoke Times*. 9 Nov. 2006.

---. "Cavs Have Officials to Thank for TD." *The Roanoke Times*. 22 Nov. 2006.

---. "Cavs Repeat the Mantra: Virginia Uses Auburn's Slogan to Beat Tigers." *The Roanoke Times*. 5 Sept. 1998.

---. "Cavs Storm Past Tigers: No. 16 Virginia 19, No. 25 Auburn 0." *The Roanoke Times*. 4 Sept. 1998.

---. "Follow the Rules and Play Ball." *The Roanoke Times*. 29 Sept. 2005.

---. "From Obscurity to Center Stage." *The Roanoke Times*. 10 Nov. 1999.

---. "Good Catch for Cavaliers -- Tight End from Small Town Makes Big Impact." *The Roanoke Times*. 4 Sept. 2002.

---. "Groh, Cavs Overcome Blue Devils 44-30." *The Roanoke Times*. 15 Oct. 1995.

---. "Groh's Cavs Full of Surprises." *The Roanoke Times*. Nov. 11, 2001.

---. "'He's a Walking Miracle.'" *The Roanoke Times*. 14 April 2005.

---. "Inspired by Brawl, Cavaliers Deck Blue Devils 35-0." *The Roanoke Times*. 26 Sept. 1993.

---. "Kick Wobbles, But Ties." *The Roanoke Times*. 19 Oct. 2008.

---. "Koshansky's Blast Gives UVa Wild Win: UVa 12, Wake Forest 11, 10 Innings." *The Roanoke Times*. 24 May 2003.

---. "Not Road Tripped." *The Roanoke Times*. 29 Jan. 2007.

---. "One More Week at No. 1? Cavaliers Run Record to 7-0 with 49-14 Win Against Deacs." *The Roanoke Times*. 21 Oct. 1990.

---. "One Slip of Paper Provided All the Inspiration." *The Roanoke Times*. 29 Jan. 1990.

---. "Reynolds Shows His Ill Will." *The Roanoke Times*. 7 Jan. 2005.

---. "Rogers Saves Best for Last." *The Roanoke Times*. 11 March 2003.

---. "Stith Rescues Cavaliers." *The Roanoke Times*. 27 Jan. 1991.

---. "Thankful for All of Life's Opportunities." *The Roanoke Times*. 29 Aug. 2010.

---. "Time Stands Still." *The Roanoke Times*. 16 Oct. 2005.

---. "UVa, Blundin Blister Tech: Cavs' QB Sets Records in 38-0 Rout." *The Roanoke Times*. 24 Nov. 1991.

---. "UVa Gave Shula a Start 50 Years Ago." *The Roanoke Times*. 19 Feb. 2008.

---. "UVa Reverses Fortune, Trounces Terrapins." *The Roanoke Times*. 5 Oct. 2008.

---. "UVa Rises from Ashes, Singes UNC." *The Roanoke Times*. 17 Nov. 1996.

---. "UVa Women Send Tennessee Home Empty-Handed." *The Roanoke Times*. 25 March 1990.

---. "Wedding Bells on a Bye Week." *The Roanoke Times*. 7 Oct. 2009.

---. "Welsh Makes Bold Call." *The Roanoke Times*. 28 Sept. 1999.

Doughty, Doug and Roland Lazenby. *'Hoos 'N' Hokies: The Rivalry: 100 Years of Virginia/Virginia Tech Football*. Dallas: Taylor Publishing Company, 1995.

Graham, Chris, and Patrick Hite. *Mad About U: Four Decades of Basketball at University Hall*. Waynesboro, VA: Augusta Free Press, 2006.

Hass, Bill. "Bill Hass on the ACC: Virginia Faces One More Challenge on Its Long Road to the College World Series." *TheACC.com*. 12 June 2009.

http://www.theacc.com/sports/m-basebl/spec-rel/061209aaa.html.

Jenkins. Jay. "Some UVA Baseball Players Have Interesting Habits." *Charlottesville Daily Progress*. 2 June 2010. http://www2.wsls.com/sports/2010/jun/02.

Jenkins, Lee. "The Education of Chris Long." *Sports Illustrated*. 10 March 2008. http://sports illustrated.cnn.com/vault/article/magazine/MAG1109935/index.html.

Keith, Larry. "Virginia Crashes the Party." *Sports Illustrated*. 15 March 1976. http://sports illustrated.cnn.com/vault/article/magazine/MAG1090846/index.htm.

Looney, Douglas S. "A Blazing Dawn." *Sports Illustrated*. 19 Nov. 1990. http://sportsillus trated.cnn.com/vault/article/magazine/MAG1136187/index.htm.

MacArthur, John. *Twelve Ordinary Men*. Nashville: W Publishing Group, 2002.

McFarling, Aaron. "Pressure-Filled -- Yes, But What a Great Reward." *The Roanoke Times*. 16 Oct. 2005.

"Men's Basketball: Cavalier Legends." *virginiasports.com*. http://www.virginiasports.com/ViewArticle.dbml?DB_OEM_ID=17800&ATCLID=204978167.

Ratcliffe, Jerry. "A Tribute to Bob Sandell." *Cavalier Insider*. 1 Feb. 2011. http://www.mydaily progress.com/index.php/crunchtime/article.

---. "Christian's Death Helped Change Game." *The Daily Progress*. 14 Nov. 2009. http://www.2.dailyprogress.com/sports/cdp-sports-cavinsider/2009/nov/14/christians_death.

---. "Honoring a Virginia Institution." *Cavalier Insider*. 8 June 2008. http://ww.2cavalier insider.com/sports/cdp-sports/2008/jun/08.

---. "Honoring a Virginia Legend." *Cavalier Insider*. 25 April 2009. http://www2.cavalier insider.com/sports/cdp-sports/2009/apr/25.

---. "Honoring a Virginia Legend." *Cavalier Insider*. 10 Oct. 2009. http://www.2cavalier insider.com/sports/cdp-sports/2009/oct/10.

---. "Sene Makes His Rare Baskets Count." *Cavalier Insider*. 20 Dec. 2010. http://www2. cavalierinsider.com/sports/2010/dec/20.

---. *The University of Virginia Football Vault: The History of the Cavaliers*. Atlanta: Whitman Publishing, LLC, 2008.

Rice, Justin A. "Spiller Delivers Knockout Blow." *The State*. 2 Nov. 2008. http://docs.news bank.com/s/InfoWeb/aggdocs/NewsBank/12434A3FE4C4F2D8.

Sumner, Jim. "Looking Back: Quayle's Drive Carried Virginia over Its Hurdle." *TheACC. com*. 15 Oct. 2008. http://www.theacc.com/sports/m-footbl/spec-rel/101508aad.html.

"Traditions: Beta and Seal." VirginiaSports.com. http://www.virginiasports.com/View Article.dbml?DB_OEM_ID=1780.

Trexel, Cayce. "Dr. Risher -- UVa's Oldesr Football Alumnus -- Turns 100." *VirginiaSports. com*. 11 May 2010. http://www.virginiasports.com/ViewArticle.dmbl?DB_OEM_ID=17800.

Uthman, Daniel. "Pass Play Lucky for UVa." *The Roanoke Times*. 24 Sept. 1995.

Walters, John. "That Cavalier Attitude." *Sports Illustrated*. 7 June 1999. http://sports illustrated.cnn.com/vault/article/magazine/MAG1016082/index.htm.

Waugh, Katrina. "Hall's Repertoire Is Growing." *The Roanoke Times*. 11 Oct. 2009."

---. "Wright, Cavs Pull Plug on Horror Flick." *The Roanoke Times*. 12 Jan. 2009.

White, Jeff. "Another Crippen Leaves Legacy at UVa." *VirginiaSports.com*. 25 Jan. 2011. http://www.virginiasports.com/ViewArticle.dbml?&ATCLID=-205082866&DB_OEM_ID=17800.

Whiteside, Kelly. "Four-peat." *Sports Illustrated*. 19 Dec. 1994. http://sportsillustrated.cnn. com/vault/article/magazine/MAG1006092/index.htm.

Wright, Kris. "Sherrill Showing Toughness." *TheSabre.com*. 3 Jan. 2011. http://www.the sabre.com/sabremail/archives/2011/sabremail0477.html.

# CAVALIERS

## INDEX OF NAMES
### (LAST NAME, FIRST NAME, DEVOTION DAY NUMBER)

Abell, Earl 21
Abrams, Mike 68
Albert, Branden 69
Alderman, Edwin 80
Alexander, Cory 38
Allen, Pete 57
Amaro, Rob 52
Arena, Bruce 5, 96
Arico, Kevin 28, 52, 92
Arnette, Gene 53
Ashe, Arthur 40, 87
Bacall, Aaron 32
Bakhtiar, Jim 99
Barber, Ronde 37
Barber, Tiki 37, 57, 60
Barkley, Charles 78
Beamer, Frank 25, 36, 81
Bennett, Tony 2
Bernardino, Mark 67
Berra, Yogi 15, 37, 83
Bestwick, Dick 4
Beta 66
Billyk, Allen 32
Bischoff, Bob 24
Blackburn, George 39
Blundin, Matt 61
Bonner, Dan 31, 41, 82
Bowden, Bobby 4, 8, 79, 86
Bowden, Terry 93, 95
Bowie, Kevin 4
Bowman, Scotty 30
Bradshaw, Terry 22
Bravo, Paul 96
Brewer, Billy 10
Brill, Bill 94
Brooks, Aaron 72
Brooks, Kevin 20
Bruno, Stephen 52
Bryant, Bear 33, 98
Burge, Heather 55, 89
Burge, Heidi 55, 58, 89
Burnim, Adrian 84
Burns, Tom 6
Butler, Brad 78
Cain, Jason 83
Capel, Jeff 38
Cardoza, Tonya 55
Carraway, Andrew 28
Causey, Jeff 5
Champ, Scott 5
Christian, Archer 80
Clark, Jason 76
Coffey, Kevin 27
Coker, Larry 40

Coleman, T.G. 75
Coles, Bimbo 46
Collins, Nate 56
Coma, Tony 19
Connelly, Jim 8
Copper, Jon 56
Corrigan, Gene 31, 39
Corso, Lee 77
Council, Walter 44
Covington, Maurice 25
Crippen, Claire 67
Crippen, Fran 67
Crocker, Joe 81
Crotty, John 46, 62, 79
Crowell, Germane 77
Crum, Dick 60
Curry, Muffin 68
Curtis, Marty 13
Curtis, Ryan 13
Davis, Bob 10, 39
Davis, Roger 10
Dawson, Fred 21
de Lench, Brooke 68
de Vivie, Paul 70
Dees, Benny 11
Dooley, Bill 42
Dudley, Bill 15, 48, 90
Dunn, Matt 100
Dunn, Warrick 84
Durham, Woody 26
Edwards, Whitny 11
Elias, Dill 10, 39, 87
Ellis, Dan 27, 72
Ellsworth, Percy 81
Eskandarian, Alecko 23
Eskandarian, Andranik 23
Evans, Dena 89
Evans, Jerton 27
Fallon, Drew 96
Ferguson, D'Brickashaw 3, 78
Fielder, Craig 64
Finkelston, Tim 29
Fisher, Mike 23
Fisher, Nikki 6
Ford, John 42
Foreman, Tyree 68
Franklin, Tony 78
Frederick, Mike 20
Fulton, Otis 35
Gamble, John 64
Garcia, Rafael 77, 81
Gillen, Pete 43, 76
Gillette, Jimmy 70

Gillispie, Paul 100
Gooch, Bobby 87
Goodman, Bobby 97
Gore, Buddy 53
Gosselin, Phil 28, 52
Grier, Andre 4
Groh, Al 3, 7, 34, 40, 47, 56, 65, 78
Groh, Mike 57, 88
Groos, Margaret 86
Guepe, Art 34, 50, 74, 85
Hagans, Marques 3, 78
Hall, Vic 7, 32
Harrell, K.T. 2, 33
Harris, Antwan 77
Hartwyk, Kevin 75
Headd, Scott 100
Henske, Tom 5
Hobgood, Jim 8
Hodges, Tom 10
Holcomb, Hanley 13
Holland, Terry 26, 31, 35, 58, 73
Hughes, Connor 78
Jackson, Bo 23
Jeffers, Patrick 88
Jeffries, Mel 14
Johnson, Jimmy 22
Johnson, Steve 29
Jones, Jeff 38, 62
Jones, Skeet 84
Jones, Thomas 27
Joseph, Adrian 83
Kelly, Barbara 31, 82
Kemp, Stan 10
Killian, P.J. 6
Kiphart, Ridlon 45
Kirby, Terry 97
Kite, Chris 64
Koch, Cary 25
Koshansky, Joe 100
Kuhn, Karl 52
Lageman, Jeff 29
Laird, Adam 100
Lambert, Casey 92
Lambeth, William 80
Lamp, Jeff 79
Langloh, Billy 35
Lawrence, Don 39
Leitao, Dave 71, 83
Levine, Ryan 52
Littles, Lyndra 11
Locke, Bobby 24
Lombardi, Vince 5,

213

# VIRGINIA

41

London, Mike 17
London, Ticynn 17
Long, Chris 22
Long, Howie 22
Lundy, Wali 3, 78
Mack, Ken 97
Mackovic, John 72
Majkowski, Don 42
Male, Evan J. 50, 94
Maravich, Pete 31
Martin, Kareem 97
Mason, Tavon 47
Mattioli, Keith 29
Mayer, Eugene 54, 75
McCue, Frank 62
McGonnigal, Bruce 6
McGugin, Dan 90
McGuire, Murray M. 98
McLeod, Rodney 56
McMullen, Billy 47, 68
Meacham, Francklyn 1
Miller, Heath 45
Minnifield, Chase 56
Molinari, Larry 10
Moore, Claude 75
Moore, Herman 6, 36
Moore, Shawn 6
Moorer, Ariana 11
Morgan, Richard 26, 46
Moseley, Frank 24
Murray, Frank 15, 90
Musgrave, Bill 47
Neal, Randy 97
Neale, Earle 14
Neely, Sidney 1
O'Connor, Brian 28, 92
Ogletree, Kevin 25
Oliver, Anthony 46, 58
Osisek, Steve 95
Paige, Leroy 57
Palmer, Wendy 89
Palumbo, Joe 85
Papit, John 53, 74, 97
Parker, Greg 52
Parker, Jarrett 52
Parkhill, Barry 8
Pearman, Alvin 47
Peerman, Cedric 25, 32, 91
Phillips, Bum 39

Pincavage, John 10
Poe, John 98
Poindexter, Anthony 84, 93
Potts, Allen 59
Proscia, Steven 52
Pyne, Jim 97
Quayle, Frank 39, 53
Randle, Sonny 63
Randolph, Robert 25
Record, Kim 73
Reiss, Tammi 55
Reynolds, J.R. 71, 76, 83
Richards, Bob 74
Risher, John 21, 34
Rivers, David 72
Robinson, Craig 16
Rodgers, Bill 54
Rogers, H. Reid 1
Rogers, Jason 43
Rosenbluth, Len 94
Ryan, Debbie 11, 19, 31, 41, 55, 58, 71, 73
Saliba, Ethan 62
Sampson, Ralph 16, 71
Sandell, Bob 65
Sax, Steve 59
Schaub, Matt 3
Schultz, Dick 9
Seal 66
Sebo, Steve 24
Secules, Scott 29
Selfridge, Andy 24
Sene, Assane 33
Sewell, Jameel 32, 40
Sharper, Jamie 84
Sherman, Tim 37, 77
Sherrill, Will 2
Shine, Chelsea 11
Shula, Don 63
Simmons, Larry 68
Simpson, Mikell 56
Sims, Ashley 69
Singletary, Sean 71, 83
Sintim, Clint 22, 91
Skinner, Al 71
Slaughter, Edward 86
Slaughter, Mary 86
Smith, Dean 26
Smith, Devin 76
Smith, Doug 79

Southern, Anthony 27
Spiller, C.J. 62
Spinner, Bryson 47, 68
St. Clair, John 27
Stadlin, Kenny 42
Staley, Dawn 19, 55
Stargell, Willie 26
Starsia, Dom 13
Stenzel, Barbara 41
Stith, Bryant 79
Strasburg, Stephen 28
Stupar, Jonathan 18
Stupar, Steve 18
Sullivan, Gilly 34, 50
Sweeney, David 6
Thurman, Allen 75
Tippett, R.E. 54
Toliver, Elton 29
Torre, Joe 28
Tranquill, Gary 27
Trevino, Lee 56
Valdes, Franco 52
Verica, Marc 25, 91
Voris, Dick 63
Walker, Herschel 34
Walker, Wally 35
Ward, Tekshia 55
Weeks, Marquis 68
Weir, Bob 34, 74
Welsh, George 6, 9, 12, 27, 29, 34, 37, 42, 57, 60, 64, 72, 88, 98
White, Todd 57, 77
Wilcox, Charles 1
Wilkinson, Buzzy 94
Williams, Kathy 41
Williams, Richie 5, 96
Willis, Symmion 20
Wilmer, Danny 60
Wolff, Dennis 89
Womack, Dennis 51, 100
Wood, A.J. 49
Wooden, John 1, 53
Woods, Brandon 56
Woods, Khama 56
Word, Barry 74
Wright, Monica 11, 19
Yorks, Lyle 5, 96
Zaharias, Babe 77
Zatopek, Emil 49